FLASHPOINT RUSSIA, Russia's Air Power: Capabilities and Structure

Piotr Butowski

FLASHPOINT RUSSIA

Russia's Air Power: Capabilities and Structure

Piotr Butowski

HARPIA PUBLISHING

Meynertgasse 8/8, 1090 Wien, Austria
enquiries@harpia-publishing.com

Consulting and inspiration by Kerstin Berger

Front cover artwork by Ugo Crisponi: The Tu-160 named *Pyotr Deynekin* was completed from an unfinished airframe remaining from the Soviet period, and was first flown in December 2017.

Rear cover artwork by Ugo Crisponi (from top to bottom): MiG-31 '81 Blue' from the 929 GLITs at Akhtubinsk; A-50U RF-93952 '45 Red' from the 610 TsBP PLS, and Mi-8MTV-2 RF-34280 '120' from Rosgvardia's 11 OAE based at Voronezh.

Editorial by Thomas Newdick

Layout by Norbert Novak, www.media-n.at, Vienna

Maps by James Lawrence, Gingercake Creative

Printed at Finidr, Czech Republic

Harpia Publishing is a member of

ISBN 978-0-9973092-7-0

Contents

Introduction

This book presents the Russian military aviation at the peak of its strength. The aviation of the Russian Ministry of Defence, i.e. the aerospace forces and navy has around 2,300 fixed-wing aircraft and almost 1,000 helicopters; other services, Rosgvardia and the FSB have in total around 100 fixed-wing aircraft and 250 helicopters.

In the decade since 2011, the Russian Armed Forces have obtained nearly 500 new fixed-wing aircraft, mostly combat types, and 700 helicopters. This is 10 times more than during 2001–10. Hundreds of combat aircraft have been upgraded. All MiG-31 interceptors, Su-24 tactical bombers, Su-25 attack aircraft, plus Tu-22M, Tu-95MS and Tu-160 heavy bombers are subject to upgrades resulting in significant enhancement of combat capabilities. In the navy, Il-38 ASW aircraft and Ka-27 helicopters are being upgraded. With minor exceptions, the MiG-29 and Su-27 fighters are not being upgraded, but replaced with new Su-30SM and Su-35S fighters. Army helicopters have already been almost completely replaced with new ones.

A worse situation exists for non-combat aircraft, where the renewal of the inventory is an exception, not the rule. Among transport aircraft, only several dozen light L-410, An-140 and An-148 staff transports are new. Since the breakup of the USSR, the air arm has not received a single new aerial tanker or early warning aircraft (apart from several A-50U upgrades); production of Il-78M-90A and A-100 aircraft is due to commence in a couple of years.

Countless military manoeuvres of various scales, including the annual strategic exercises Kavkaz ('Caucasus'), Tsentr ('Centre'), Vostok ('East') or Zapad ('West'), as well as participation in the expeditionary campaign in Syria since autumn 2015, have given the aerospace forces the opportunity to gain experience and improve both the equipment and the command system as well as personnel skills. Most Russian pilots and air commanders have gone through the Syrian theatre.

Such a decade will not be repeated. Russia has entered a period of protracted crisis. The country's defence spending peaked in 2015, but then began to decline; in real terms the fall is almost 20 per cent between 2015 and 2018.

Two values characterise military spending in Russia: the spending under the 'national defence' budget chapter, comprised mainly of funding for defence-ministry forces (this number is officially given by Russia), and the total military expenditure as calculated according to the standard NATO definition, including other budget chapters. According to the first data, military spending in Russia in 2018 amounted to USD46 billion or 2.9 per cent of the national Global Domestic Product (GDP); according to the second, it was USD63.1 billion or 4.0 per cent of GDP (estimates from the IISS Military Balance 2019 yearbook). In relation to GDP it is twice as much as most NATO countries spend (apart from the United States, at 3.1 per cent); however, it must be remembered that the economic potential of the NATO countries is some 15 times greater than the Russian economy.

Reduced military spending should be viewed against the background of a faltering Russian economy after a drop in oil prices. The Russian economy is still a single-parameter one and the oil price is this parameter. As the increase of Russian military potential after 2000 resulted from high oil prices lasting for a whole decade, the reduction in military spending after 2014 is the result of the slump in oil prices in autumn 2014. The price of a barrel of Brent oil is currently USD70, compared with an average USD110 in 2012–13.

Acknowledgments

This is the fourth book in the 'Russian' series from Harpia Publishing. It presents the organisational structure and quantitative potential of Russian military aviation. All aircraft, helicopters and other flying vehicles operated by Russia's military aviation, their technical characteristics and combat capabilities are presented in the first two books. The third book describes Russia's air-launched weapons.

The main body of this book is a description of the structure and units of Russian military aviation. Many orders of battle have already been published in the past; not all of them are reliable. This book is a completely original work; every sentence has been written anew, all information has been checked carefully as much as possible. Google Earth, providing access to satellite photographs, has proven an invaluable aid in determing the stationing of air units.

Kisses to my loved ones, Irina, Joanna, Mark and Filip.

Abbreviations

Abbreviation	Russian term (in Latin)	Russian term (in Cyrillic)	English term
AvB	Aviatsionnaya baza	Авиационная база	Aviation Base
A VVS PVO	Armiya Voyenno-vozdushnykh sil i Protivovozdushnoy oborony	Армия Военно-воздушных сил и Противовоздушной обороны	Air Force and Air Defence Army
ADON	Aviatsionnaya diviziya osobogo naznacheniya	Авиационная дивизия особого назначения	Aviation Division of Special Purpose
AEPSO	Aviatsionnaya eskadrilya poiskovo-spasatelnogo obespecheniya	Авиационная эскадрилья поисково-спасательного обеспечения	Aviation Squadron of Search and Rescue Providing
AOSN	Aviatsionnyi otryad spetsialnogo naznacheniya	Авиационный отряд специального назначения	Aviation Detachments of Special Purpose
AvB AA	Aviatsionnaya baza Armeyskoi aviatsii	Авиационная база Армейской авиации	Aviation Base of Army Aviation
AvGr	Aviatsionnaya gruppa	Авиационная группа	Aviation Group
AvK	Aviatsionnaya komendatura	Авиационная комендатура	Duty Post
BAP	Bombardirovochnyi aviatsionnyi polk	Бомбардировочный авиационный полк	Bomber Aviation Regiment
BATO	Batalyon aerodromno-tekhnicheskogo obespecheniya	Батальон аэродромно-технического обеспечения	Battalion of Airfield and Technical Maintenance
Br AA	Brigada Armeyskoi aviatsii	Бригада Армейской авиации	Army Aviation Brigade
BS RTO	Batalyon svyazi i radiotekhnicheskogo obespecheniya	Батальон связи и радиотехнического обеспечения	Battalion of Communication and Radio Support
DA	Dalnyaya aviatsiya	Дальняя авиация	Long-Range Aviation
FSB	Federalnaya sluzhba bezopasnosti	Федеральная служба безопасности	Federal Security Service
FSO	Federalnaya sluzhba okhrany	Федеральная служба охраны	Federal Guard Service
GLITs MO RF	Gosudarstvennyi lyotno-ispytatelnyi tsentr Ministerstva oborony Rossiyskoy Federatsii	Государственный лётно-испытательный центр Министерства обороны Российской Федерации	State Flight-Test Centre of Ministry of Defence of the Russian Federation
GOU	Glavnoye operativnoye upravleniye	Главное оперативное управление	Main Operations Directorate
GOZ	Gosudarstvennyi oboronnyi zakaz	Государственный оборонный заказ	State Defence Order
GPV	Gosudarstvennaya programma vooruzheniya	Государственная программа вооружения	State Armament Program
GSh	Generalnyi shtab	Генеральный штаб	General Staff
GTs BA MO RF	Gosudarstvennyi tsentr bespilotnoy aviatsii Ministerstva oborony Rossiyskoy Federatsii	Государственный центр беспилотной авиации Министерства обороны Российской Федерации	State Unmanned Aircraft Centre of Ministry of Defence of the Russian Federation
GTs PAP VI MO RF	Gosudarstvennyi tsentr podgotovki aviatsionnogo personala i voyskovykh ispytaniy Ministerstva oborony Rossiyskoy Federatsii	Государственный центр подготовки авиационного персонала и войсковых испытаний Министерства обороны Российской Федерации	State Air Personnel Preparation and Military Evaluation Centre of Ministry of Defence of the Russian Federation
IAP	Istrebitelnyi aviatsionnyi polk	Истребительный авиационный полк	Fighter Aviation Regiment
IAS	Inzhenerno-aviatsionnaya sluzhba	Инженерно-авиационная служба	Engineering Aviation Service
IIVE	Issledovatelskaya instruktorskaya vertolyotnaya eskadrilya	Исследовательская инструкторская вертолётная эскадрилья	Research Instructor Helicopter Squadron
IIVP	Issledovatelskiy instruktorskiy vertolyotnyi polk	Исследовательский инструкторский вертолётный полк	Research Instructor Helicopter Regiment
KIAD	Korabelnaya istrebitelnaya aviatsionnaya diviziya	Корабельная истребительная авиационная дивизия	Shipborne Fighter Aviation Division
KIAP	Korabelnyi istrebitelnyi aviatsionnyi polk	Корабельный истребительный авиационный полк	Shipborne Fighter Aviation Regiment
KP	Komandnyi Punkt	Командный пункт	Command Post
KV	Kosmicheskiye voyska	Космические войска	Space Troops
KVVAUL	Krasnodarskoye vyssheye voyennoye aviatsionnoye uchilishche lyotchikov	Краснодарское высшее военное авиационное училище лётчиков	Krasnodar Military Aviation College for Pilots
MA VMF	Morskaya aviatsiya Voenno-morskogo flota	Морская авиация Военно-морского Флота	Naval Aviation of the Navy
MO	Ministerstvo oborony	Министерство обороны	Ministry of Defence

MShAP	Morskoy shturmovoy aviatsionnyi polk	Морской штурмовой авиационный полк	Naval Attack Aviation Regiment
NTsUO	Natsionalnyi tsentr upravleniya oboronoy	Национальный центр управления обороной	National Defence Management Centre
OAE	Otdelnaya aviatsionnaya eskadrilya	Отдельная авиационная эскадрилья	Independent Aviation Squadron
OAP DRLO	Otdelnyi aviatsionnyi polk dalnego radiolokatsionnogo obnaruzheniya	Отдельный авиационный полк дальнего радиолокационного обнаружения	Independent Aviation Regiment of Long-Range Radar Surveillance
OAP SZ	Otdelnyi aviatsionnyi polk samolotov zapravshchikov	Отдельный авиационный полк самолётов заправщиков	Independent Tanker Aviation Regiment
OBAP	Otdelnyi bombardirovochnyi aviatsionnyi polk	Отдельный бомбардировочный авиационный полк	Independent Bomber Aviation Regiment
ODRAO	Otdelnyi dalniy razvedyvatelnyi aviatsionnyi otryad	Отдельный дальний разведывательный авиационный отряд	Independent Long-range Reconnaissance Aviation Detachment
OE BLA	Otdelnaya eskadrilya bespilotnykh letatelnykh apparatov	Отдельная эскадрилья беспилотных летательных аппаратов	Independent Unmanned Aerial Vehicles Squadron
OIAP	Otdelnyi istrebitelnyi aviatsionnyi polk	Отдельный истребительный авиационный полк	Independent Fighter Aviation Regiment
OKIAP	Otdelnyi korabelnyi istrebitelnyi aviatsionnyi polk	Отдельный корабельный истребительный авиационный полк	Independent Shipborne Fighter Aviation Regiment
OKPLVE	Otdelnaya korabelnaya protivolodochnaya vertolyotnaya eskadrilya	Отдельная корабельная противолодочная вертолетная эскадрилья	Independent Shipborne ASW Helicopter Squadron
OMShAP	Otdelnyi morskoy shturmovoy aviatsionnyi polk	Отдельный морской штурмовой авиационный полк	Independent Naval Attack Aviation Regiment
OP BLA	Otdelnyi polk bespilotnykh letatelnykh apparatov	Отдельный полк беспилотных летательных аппаратов	Independent Unmanned Aerial Vehicles Regiment
OPLAE	Otdelnaya protivolodochnaya aviatsionnaya eskadrilya	Отдельная противолодочная авиационная эскадрилья	Independent ASW Aviation Squadron
ORAP	Otdelnyi razvedyvatelnyi aviatsionnyi polk	Отдельный разведывательный авиационный полк	Independent Reconnaissance Aviation Regiment
OSAE	Otdelnaya smeshannaya aviatsionnaya eskadrilya	Отдельная смешанная авиационная эскадрилья	Independent Composite Aviation Squadron
OSAP	Otdelnyi smeshannyi aviatsionnyi polk	Отдельный смешанный авиационный полк	Independent Composite Aviation Regiment
OShAP	Otdelnyi shturmovoy aviatsionnyi polk	Отдельный штурмовой авиационный полк	Independent Attack Aviation Regiment
OSK	Obyedinyonnoye strategicheskoye komandovaniye	Объединённое стратегическое командование	Joint Strategic Command
OTAE	Otdelnaya transportnaya aviatsionnaya eskadrilya	Отдельная транспортная авиационная эскадрилья	Independent Transport Aviation Squadron
OTAP	Otdelnyi transportnyi aviatsionnyi polk	Отдельный транспортный авиационный полк	Independent Transport Aviation Regiment
OTBVP	Otdelnyi transportno-boyevoy vertoliotnyi polk	Отдельный транспортно-боевой вертолётный полк	Independent Transport-Combat Helicopter Regiment
OTSAP	Otdelnyi transportnyi smeshannyi aviatsionnyi polk	Отдельный транспортный смешанный авиационный полк	Independent Transport Composite Aviation Regiment
OVE	Otdelnaya vertolyotnaya eskadrilya	Отдельная вертолетная эскадрилья	Independent Helicopter Squadron
OVP	Otdelnyi vertoliotnyi polk	Отдельный вертолётный полк	Independent Helicopter Regiment
OVTAE	Otdelnaya voyenno-transportnaya aviatsionnaya eskadrilya	Отдельная военно-транспортная авиационная эскадрилья	Independent Military Transport Aviation Squadron
RAP	Razvedyvatelnyi aviatsionnyi polk	Разведывательный авиационный полк	Reconnaissance Aviation Regiment
RVSN	Raketnye voyska strategicheskogo naznacheniya	Ракетные войска стратегического назначения	Strategic Rocket Troops
SAD	Smeshannaya aviatsionnaya diviziya	Смешанная авиационная дивизия	Composite Aviation Division
SAP	Smeshannyi aviatsionnyi polk	Смешанный авиационный полк	Composite Aviation Regiment
SAP(ON)	Smeshannyi aviatsionnyi polk (osobogo naznacheniya)	Смешанный авиационный полк (особого назначения)	Composite Aviation Regiment (Special Purpose)
ShAP	Shturmovoy aviatsionnyi polk	Штурмовой авиационный полк	Attack Aviation Regiment
SV	Sukhoputnyje voyska	Сухопутные войска	Ground Troops

TBAD	Tyazholaya bombardirovochnaya aviatsionnaya diviziya	Тяжёлая бомбардировочная авиационная дивизия	Heavy Bomber Aviation Division
TBAP	Tyazholyi bombardirovochnyi aviatsionnyi polk	Тяжёлый бомбардировочный авиационный полк	Heavy Bomber Aviation Regiment
TECh	Tekhniko-ekspluatatsionnaya chast'	Технико-эксплуатационная часть	Technical Operational Unit
TsBP BPr	Tsentr boyevoy podgotovki i boyevogo primeneniya	Центр боевой подготовки и боевого применения	Combat Training and Combat Application Centre
TsBP PLS	Tsentr boyevoy podgotovki i pereuchivaniya lyotnogo sostava	Центр боевой подготовки и переучивания лётного состава	Combat Training and Flight Crew Conversion Centre
TsBP PLS AA	TsBP PLS Armeyskoy aviatsii	ЦБП ПЛС Армейской авиации	TsBP PLS of Army Aviation
TsBP PLS DA	TsBP PLS Dalney aviatsii	ЦБП ПЛС Дальней авиации	TsBP PLS of Long-Range Aviation
TsBP PLS MA	TsBP PLS Morskoy aviatsii	ЦБП ПЛС Морской авиации	TsBP PLS of Naval Aviation
TsBP PLS VTA	TsBP PLS Voyenno-transportnoy aviatsii	ЦБП ПЛС Военно-транспортной авиации	TsBP PLS of Military Transport Aviation
TsNII MO RF	Tsentralnyi nauchno-issledovatelskiy institute Ministerstva oborony Rossiyskoy Federatsii	Центральный научно-исследовательский институт Министерства обороны Российской Федерации	Central Research Institute of the Ministry of Defence of Russian Federation
TsNII VVS MO RF	Tsentralnyi nauchno-issledovatelskiy institut Voyenno-vozdushnikh sil MO RF	Центральный научно-исследовательский институт Военно-воздушных сил Министерства обороны Российской Федерации	Central Research Institute of the Air Force of Ministry of Defence of Russian Federation
TsPAT	Tsentr pokaza aviatsionnoy tekhniki	Центр показа авиационной техники	Aviation Technology Demonstration Centre
UAvB	Uchebnaya aviatsionnaya baza	Учебная авиационная база	Training Aviation Base
UAP	Uchebnyi aviatsionnyi polk	Учебный авиационный полк	Training Aviation Regiment
USAP	Uchebnyi smeshannyi aviatsionnyi polk	Учебный смешанный авиационный полк	Training Composite Aviation Regiment
UTsBPr	Uchebnyi tsentr boyevogo primeneniya	Учебный центр боевого применения	Combat Application Training Centre
VDV	Vozdushno-desantnye voyska	Воздушно-десантные войска	Airborne Troops
VGK	Verkhovnoye glavnokomandovaniye	Верховное главнокомандование	Supreme High Command
VKS	Vozdushno-kosmicheskiye sily	Воздушно-космические силы	Aerospace Forces
VMF	Voyenno-morskoy flot	Военно-морской флот	Navy
VO	Voyennyi okrug	Военный округ	Military District
VP	Vertoliotnyi polk	Вертолётный полк	Helicopter Regiment
VPK	Voyenno-promyshlennaya komissiya	Военно-промышленная комиссия	Military-Industrial Commission
V PVO	Voyska Protivovozdushnoy oborony	Войска Противовоздушной обороны	Air Defence Troops
V PVO PRO	Voyska protivovozdushnoy i protivoraketnoy oborony	Войска противовоздушной и противоракетной обороны	Air and Missile Defence Troops
VTA	Voyenno-transportnaya aviatsiya	Военно-транспортная авиация	Military Transport Aviation
VTAD	Voyenno-transportnaya aviatsionnaya diviziya	Военно-транспортная авиационная дивизия	Military Transport Aviation Division
VTAP	Voyenno-transportnyi aviatsionnyi polk	Военно-транспортный авиационный полк	Military Transport Aviation Regiment
VVS	Voyenno-vozdushnye sily	Военно-воздушные силы	Air Force
VUNTs VVS ‚VVA'	Voyennyi uchebno-nauchnyi tsentr VVS ‚Voyenno-vozdushnaya akademiya'	Военный учебно-научный центр ВВС «Военно-воздушная академия»	Air Force Military Educational and Scientific Centre ‚Air Force Academy'
VzPU VS RF	Vozdushnyi punkt upravleniya Vooruzhennymi silami RF	Воздушный пункт управления Вооруженными силами Российской Федерации	Airborne Control Post of the Armed Forces of Russian Federation

Note: To be accurate only abbreviations of tactical and strategic formations (independent regiments, divisions, brigades and armies)should be capitalized for example TBAD or ORAP. Abbreviations of units and sub-units (regiment, squadron) in military documents are written in lower case for example iap tbap and not IAP TBAP.
However, for the needs of this book to avoid additional confusion I decided to write all abbreviations in capital letters.

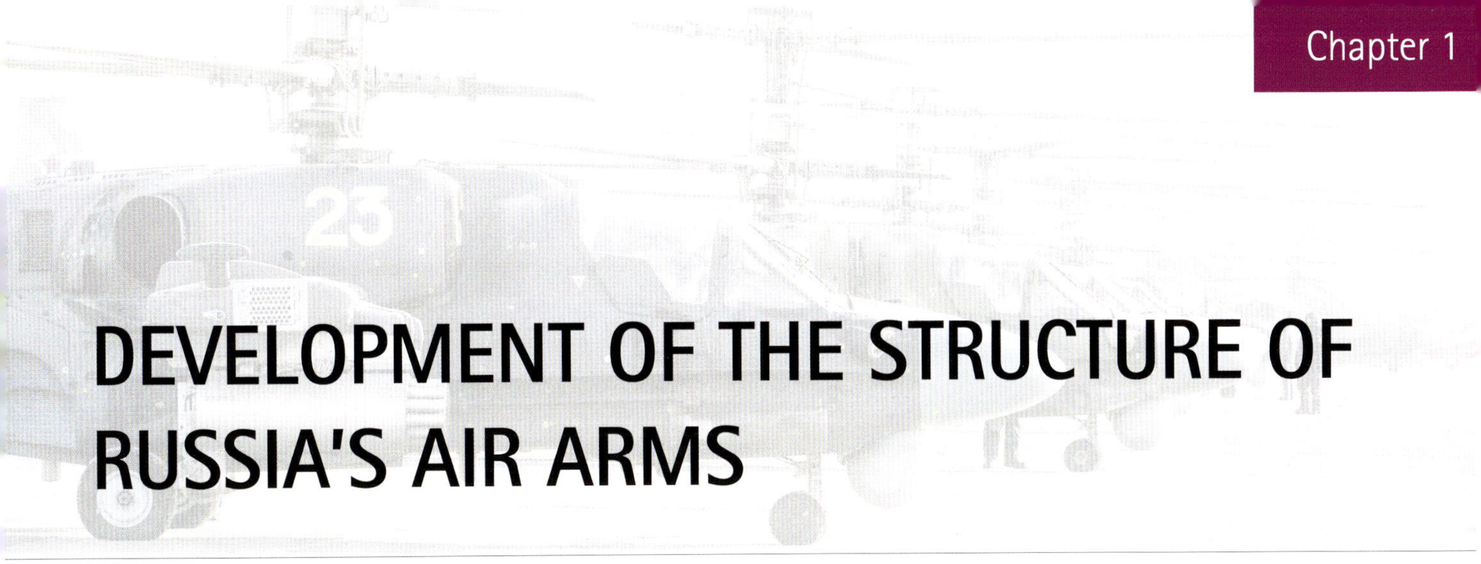

DEVELOPMENT OF THE STRUCTURE OF RUSSIA'S AIR ARMS

Russian military aviation has undergone a process of transformation in the post-Soviet era, the effects of which have been sometimes profound. The process that has created today's Russian arms can be better understood with reference to certain key dates, as follows.

Relocations after the disintegration of the USSR

In December 1991 the Union of Soviet Socialist Republics (USSR) broke up into 15 new states, each of which began to organise its own armed forces. Delaying this process was in Russia's best interests, and Moscow began to carry out advantageous translocations of troops, under the pretext that the ex-Soviet armed forces still shared commonality. The Russian Federation's armed forces were formally created on 7 May 1992.

In this initial period, the Russian air arm's most important task was to take over as many Soviet air units as possible. In Soviet times, less than 40 per cent of all combat aircraft were stationed in Russian territory. Moreover, these were generally the oldest aircraft, as the most advanced types were always first deployed in the border regions. Russia took control of and returned to its territory all Soviet air units from Eastern Europe, including the powerful 16th Air Army from East Germany and the 4th Air Army from Poland. Russia took all aircraft from the Baltic States (Estonia, Latvia and Lithuania), most of those from the Caucasian republics (Georgia and Azerbaijan), as well as some units from Belarus (Su-24M and Tu-22M bombers). Kazakhstan retained the tactical aviation assets but passed on 40 Tu-95MS strategic bombers to Russia. As a result of these measures, by 1993 Russia had in its possession around two-thirds of the military aviation of the former USSR.

Sometimes aircraft were transferred to Russia under interstate agreements (for example with Belarus and Kazakhstan), but in other instances they simply took off from their bases and did not return. In this way, the 60th Attack Aviation Regiment (ShAP, Shturmovoy aviatsionnyi polk) with Su-25 aircraft, based at Sital-chay; the 82nd Fighter Aviation Regiment (IAP, Istrebitelnyi aviatsionnyi polk) with MiG-25PDS aircraft based at Nasosnyi; and the 976th Bomber Aviation Regiment (BAP, Bombardirovochnyi aviatsionnyi polk) with Su-24s based at Kurdamir all flew from Azerbaijan to Russia. Withdrawal of the 882nd Reconnaissance Aviation Regiment (RAP, Razvedyvatelnyi aviatsionnyi polk), operating MiG-25RB and Su-24MR aircraft from Dallyar in western Azerbaijan, began on 9 June 1992. Only eight MiG-25s had managed to take off before a force of several hundred Azeri soldiers entered the airfield, blocking the runway and seizing the remaining 16 MiG-25 and Su-24 aircraft.

On 14 February 1992 six Su-24Ms from the 7 BAP based at Starokonstiantyniv, Ukraine, whose pilots did not want to join the armed forces of Ukraine, flew to Smolensk in Russia.

Redeployment of so many air units to Russia resulted in numerous difficulties both logistical and social. Air bases for the numerous new aircraft and accommodation for the personnel had to be found. This could be accomplished only by overcrowding of the existing locations. Often the regiments were disbanded after arrival in Russia and their aircraft divided among other units. The bases of the flying schools at Orenburg and Yeysk were taken over to meet the needs of the operational forces. The schools were replaced by two divisions: a transport aviation division, redeployed from the Baltic States to Orenburg, and a bomber aviation division (three Su-24 regiments) that moved from Belarus to Yeysk. The transformation of the flying schools at Orenburg (near the border with Kazakhstan) and Yeysk (on the Sea of Azov) into operational units was concurrent with plans to provide additional cover for Russia's southern flank, which had been weakened by the withdrawal of units from the Caucasian republics. All in all, these redeployments lacked strategic foresight; the units were transferred to locations that were vacant.

Air Force absorbs Air Defence Troops

The 'Soviet' organisational structure of Russian military aviation, in which air assets were divided between the Air Force (Voyenno-vozdushnye sily, VVS), Air Defence Troops (Voyska Protivovozdushnoy oborony, V PVO), Ground Troops (Sukhoputnyje voyska, SV) and the Navy (Voyenno-morskoy flot, VMF) remained unchanged for several years after the break-up of the USSR. The first thorough reform was conducted in 1998, when the majority of the Air Defence Troops, including all aircraft, surface-to-air missiles (SAMs) and the airspace radar surveillance network were transferred to the Air Force. The remainder of the V PVO, i.e. the ballistic missile warning system, Moscow's missile defence corps and space control network were integrated into the Strategic Rocket Troops (Raketnye voyska strategicheskogo naznacheniya, RVSN), before being transferred in March 2001 to the newly established Space Troops (from 2011 the Aerospace Defence Troops; since 2015 part of the Aerospace Forces).

A decree from the President of Russia, Boris Yeltsin, dated 16 July 1997 served as the formal document ordering integration of part of the V PVO into the VVS. The new structure duly came into force on 1 January 1999. Before the reform the entire Air Force command was replaced; on 20 January 1998 Colonel General Anatoly Kornukov, previously in command of the Moscow PVO District, became the new commander-in-chief (C-in-C). Reportedly, the previous C-in-C, General of the Army Pyotr Deynekin, did not agree with the planned move of VVS headquarters, after integration, to the settlement of Zarya near Balashikha, 20km (12 miles) northeast of the centre of Moscow, where the Central Command Post of the V PVO had previously been located. Additionally, lower-level staffs were usually located in previous PVO, rather than VVS command posts, due to the fact that the PVO forces were better equipped with automatic operational and combat command systems, as well as communication systems. Before the integration in the VVS, only the Long-Range Aviation (DA, Dalnyaya aviatsiya) had such systems.

The main objective of the merger of the VVS and V PVO was to reduce operational costs; following the merger, many units and commands were simply disbanded. Before the reform the VVS had 95 regiments and the Air Defence Troops 25 aviation regiments. From 1 January 1999, 70 aviation regiments remained in the new air force, including seven heavy bomber regiments, one aerial tanker aircraft regiment, 10 transport regiments, 24 fighter regiments, 11 bomber regiments, seven attack regiments, five reconnaissance regiments, five auxiliary transport aviation regiments, as well as 30 SAM regiments. The Air Force vacated 32 airfields and 310 housing estates. The planned strength of the Air Force was set at 184,594 servicemen; before the reform the VVS and V PVO had jointly numbered around 230,000.

Eight armies were subordinated to the HQ of the Air Force, as well as some direct reporting units (test and evaluation centres, pilot schools, scientific institutes, repair plants and storage bases). Two air armies were created according to functional principle: the 37th Air Army included long-range bombers and tankers, while the 61st Air Army operated strategic transport aircraft. Six VVS PVO armies were created according to territorial principle and joined the tactical air units stationed in the appropriate military districts. These were the 4th VVS PVO Army with its HQ in Rostov-on-Don; 5th Army in Yekaterinburg; 6th Army in St Petersburg; 11th Army in Khabarovsk; 14th Army in Novosibirsk; and Special Operations Command (until October 2002 the Moscow District of VVS and PVO), with HQ in Moscow, protecting Russia's capital.

Changing status of Army Aviation

On 1 January 2003, Army Aviation (combat and transport helicopters), which formerly belonged to the Ground Troops, was subordinated to the Air Force; the Russian ground forces have had no organic air assets since then. Whether helicopters should be assigned to the army or air force is still a point of discussion in Russia. During the Soviet era the Army Aviation was subordinated to the Air Force. In 1990, influenced by the experience of the war in Afghanistan (1979–89) army aviation was transferred to the Ground Troops. The decision to transfer it back to the Air Force in 2003 was made in the wake of the downing of a Mi-26 transport helicopter with the death of 119 people in Chechnya on 19 August 2002.

The investigation revealed numerous instances of negligence and weaknesses in the command of the Army Aviation within the Ground Troops. For example, it took 1.5 hours for the duty officer at the Army Aviation HQ in Moscow to make contact with a helicopter regiment in the Far East; the duty officer of the Air Force HQ managed to do it in five minutes. On 2 September 2002 the defence minister ordered transfer of the Army Aviation to the Air Force and the commanding officer of the former, Colonel General Vitaly Pavlov, was dismissed.

Currently, helicopter brigades and regiments have a dual dependence. Operationally they are managed by the Joint Strategic Commands of their respective military districts, while training and combat preparation is conducted by the Aerospace Forces. The Aerospace Forces' HQ includes a department responsible for Army Aviation combat preparation, headed by Major General Oleg Chesnokov.

A new look

The economist Anatoly Serdyukov was appointed Russian Minister of Defence on 15 February 2007. At a meeting of the ministry's board on 14 October the following year he announced plans for a thorough reform of Russia's armed forces, commonly termed the 'Novyi Oblik' (New Look). 'Serdyukov's reform' is now usually associated with the critical shortfalls revealed in the Russian military by the war with Georgia in August 2008. Although the experiences of that conflict accelerated the changes and increased the determination for their introduction, work on these plans had actually commenced earlier. The New Look programme aimed to transform the Soviet-style Russian Armed Forces into a smaller, more modern, and combat-ready military.

The number of military districts was reduced from six to four. Within the Air Force, the previous six VVS PVO armies were transformed into four VVS PVO commands, 'tied' to the new military districts (MDs): the 1st Command at Voronezh in the Western MD; 2nd Command at Yekaterinburg in the Central MD; the 3rd Command at Khabarovsk in the Eastern MD; and the 4th Command at Rostov-on-Don in the Southern MD. Strategic bombers and heavy transport aircraft were placed under the newly established Long-Range Aviation Command (the former 37th Air Army) and Military Transport Aviation Command (the former 61st Air Army), respectively.

At a lower level, the regiments, independent squadrons and detachments were transformed into 'air bases'. This was not just a simple renaming; when a new base was formed, the air unit was merged with auxiliary units stationed at the same garrison, which had previously been independent and had their own commands (battalions for airfield and technical maintenance, communication and radio support). The concentration of command of all the base's sub-units within a single headquarters reduced the number of command personnel.

The reform was poorly prepared, and plans were changed during its implementation, sometimes quite radically. First, in 2009, 72 regiments, 14 air bases plus 12 independent squadrons and detachments were re-established to create 33 air bases; initially, the planned number was 52, but this was reduced during the reorganisation. In 2010 they were reformed again, and the entire Air Force was grouped within seven large Aviation Bases 1st Grade and eight Aviation Bases 2nd Grade (five of these were Army Aviation bases and three were foreign air bases in Armenia, Kyrgyzstan and Tajikistan). An Aviation Base 1st Grade, which was the size of a former division, consisted of several aviation groups based at various airfields, each group comprising several squadrons. An Aviation Base 2nd Grade was the size of a former regiment and was based at a single airfield.

The seven Aviation Bases 1st Grade comprised four bases within the tactical aviation branch, one in each territorial command (the 7000 AvB at Voronezh in the 1st Command, 6980 AvB at Chelyabinsk in the 2nd Command, 6983 AvB at Khurba in the 3rd Command and 6972 AvB at Krymsk in the 4th Command), two long-range aviation bases (the 6950 AvB at Engels and 6952 AvB at Ukrainka) and one transport aviation base (the 6955 AvB at Tver).

During the Soviet era, tactical aviation regiments had three squadrons of combat aircraft each. In the early 2000s the third and sometimes the second squadrons 'atrophied' – there was simply no money for aircraft overhauls. During Serdyukov's reform, the number of units was reduced, and all airworthy aircraft were assigned to the remaining units, whose full assigned complements were restored. For instance, in the 4th Command there were previously two MiG-29 fighter regiments, the 31 IAP at Zernograd and 19 IAP at Millerovo; now all airworthy aircraft were transferred to Millerovo, creating an aviation group of the 6972 AvB. Likewise, in the 3rd Command in the Far East of Russia the Su-25 attack aircraft from the 18 ShAP (Galenki) and 187 ShAP (Chernigovka) were grouped into an aviation group of the 6983 AvB at Chernigovka. In some cases, units of various aircraft types were merged; for instance, the MiG-31 fighters from the disbanded 530 IAP (Chuguyevka) were transferred to Tsentralnaya Uglovaya, where they were incorporated into the aviation group of the 6983 AvB along with Su-27 fighters. Concentration of all combat-capable aircraft at a smaller number of airfields allowed for increased-intensity training with reduced costs.

Further upheavals affected Army Aviation. In 2009 the helicopters were assigned to 'regular' air bases, along with fixed-wing aircraft. For example, the Budyonnovsk base had Su-25 attack aircraft and Mi-8, Mi-24 and Mi-28N helicopters under one command, while the Domna aviation base had MiG-29 fighters and Su-25 attack aircraft, plus Mi-8 and Mi-24 helicopters. It soon proved a mistake, and since 2010 the helicopters have been organised into separate Aviation Bases of Army Aviation (AvB AA).

The Air Force also took charge of several units from the Naval Aviation. Due to the chaos of the previous reorganisation of 1998, a Su-27 fighter regiment in the Kaliningrad District (the 689 IAP based at Chkalovsk) and a MiG-31 interceptor regiment on Kamchatka (the 865 IAP based at Yelizovo) were transferred from the Air Force to Naval Aviation. In 2011 they returned to the Air Force – but not for long; as result of further changes, both units were transferred back to Naval Aviation in 2013.

On the other hand, in 2011 the Navy lost its Tu-22M3 medium bombers – once the primary air weapon against US aircraft carriers – for good. The Tu-22M3s from Mongokhto naval air base on the Pacific coast were transferred to the Air Force's Belaya air base near Irkutsk. The bombers from Olenyegorsk naval air base on the Barents Sea coast remained there but were subordinated to the Air Force.

2012: a step back

A new defence minister, Sergey Shoygu, assumed office on 6 November 2012. He ordered a study of the suitability of the structures introduced after 2008. One of the objectives of the reform of 2008 had been to simplify the command system by reducing the number of command levels. In fact, the new structure appeared too rigid. In the Air Force, its main shortcoming were the great distances between aviation groups belonging to the same aviation base – this made it difficult for the base command to manage them. The most prominent example was the 7000 AvB, whose aviation groups were dispersed across many hundreds of kilometres; the most remote group at Monchegorsk was 1,850km (1,150 miles) away from the base HQ at Voronezh.

Therefore, beginning in 2012, the aviation groups began to be given independence again and were transformed into regiments, while the headquarters of Aviation Bases 1st Grade were transformed into HQs of aviation divisions. Emotive reasons played a role, too; since 1938, Russian airmen had served in regiments and divisions, not aviation bases and groups. Many units regained their previous numbers, dating from before Serdyukov's reform. The changes were gradual and within several years the Air Force returned to its traditional structure of regiments and divisions.

On 1 November 2015 the previous territorial VVS and PVO commands were reorganised into four Air Force and Air Defence Armies: the 4th Army in Rostov-on-Don (the former 4th Command), 6th Army in St Petersburg (former 1st Command), 11th Army in Khabarovsk (former 3rd Command) and 14th Army in Yekaterinburg (former 2nd Command).

This organisational 'correction' does not imply that Serdyukov's reform was reversed; in fact, most of the changes introduced after 2008 remained permanently in force. In particular, the internal structure of the main organisational unit of the Russian military aviation, the aviation regiment, remained as in the Aviation Base 2nd Grade; for example, battalion of airfield and technical maintenance (Batalyon aerodromno-tekhnicheskogo obespecheniya, BATO) and battalion of communication and radio support (Batalyon svyazi i radiotekhnicheskogo obespecheniya, BS RTO) maintenance sub-units did not regain the independence they had before 2009. Furthermore, the stationing of air units changed only slightly; the units were not transferred back to the bases they once occupied.

The next frontier

On 1 August 2015, Russia created the Aerospace Forces (Vozdushno-kosmicheskiye sily, VKS) by merging the former Air Force and Aerospace Defence Troops (a formal decree had been issued by the Russian president on 26 February 2015). This represents the next stage in the integration of aviation and space assets under a unified organisational structure after the merger of the VVS and V PVO in 1998 and provides a counter to the US Prompt Global Strike programme. Colonel General Viktor Bondaryev, the former head of the VVS, was appointed the first C-in-C of the VKS.

In this way, aviation, air defence, Moscow's anti-ballistic missile defence as well as a constellation of around 130 spacecraft in orbit – both civilian and military –were integrated within the VKS. The aviation element of the VKS, the subject of this book, can perform in-space strikes against satellites to disrupt enemy military control, communications or information support. Flight tests of a MiG-31 armed with an anti-satellite missile began in September 2018. The advantage of an airborne anti-satellite system over a ground-based system is its longer range: a MiG-31 can carry a missile over a distance of up to 1,000km (621 miles) before launch.

AVIATION ASSETS IN RUSSIA'S MILITARY STRUCTURES

According to official doctrine, the Russian Armed Forces (Vooruzhonnyye Sily, VS) have two tasks. The first is to prevent an aggressor from attacking Russia by maintaining strategic nuclear forces, capable of destroying any such enemy. The document states that 'the Russian Federation reserves the right to use nuclear weapons in response to the use of nuclear and other types of weapons of mass destruction against it and (or) its allies, as well as in response to aggression against the Russian Federation that utilises conventional weapons that threatens the very existence of the state.' It is worth noting that, according to official doctrine, the USSR guaranteed that it would not use nuclear weapons first and not against an enemy that did not possess nuclear weapons.

The second task of the VS is to prevent a regional or local aggressor by maintaining the necessary combat potential of general-purpose forces.

The third task, not mentioned in official documents, but implemented in practice, is expanding the influence and territories subordinated to Russia by offensive actions. Currently Russia controls parts of territories of other nations: Georgia (Abkhazia and South Ossetia), Moldova (Transnistria) and Ukraine (Crimea and Donbass). With the consent of these nations, Russia also maintains bases in Armenia, Kyrgyzstan and Tajikistan, and there is a Russian military contingent fighting in Syria.

Russia's military leadership

The **Supreme High Command** (Verkhovnoye glavnokomandovaniye, VGK) is responsible for preparation and carrying out military campaigns and strategic operations. The supreme commander-in-chief of the Russian Armed Forces is President Vladimir Putin.

The **Ministry of Defence** (Ministerstvo oborony, MO) is responsible for everyday management of the armed forces. The minister of defence is Sergey Shoygu (since November 2012), who previously headed the Ministry of Emergency Situations (formally the Ministry of the Russian Federation for Affairs for Civil Defence, Emergencies and Elimination of Consequences of Natural Disasters). The headquarters of the MO, as well as of the General Staff, is located in Moscow, at Frunzenskaya Naberezhnaya (Frunze Embankment).

The **General Staff** (Generalnyi shtab, GSh) directly commands military branches and corps. The chief of the General Staff and the first deputy minister of defence is General of the Army Valery Gerasimov (since November 2012).

The **Main Operations Directorate** (Glavnoye operativnoye upravleniye, GOU) of the General Staff is responsible for defining the military threats to Russia and providing the main directions for the composition of the armed forces. It organises strategic and operational planning of the forces' use; executes operational management of troops in peacetime and wartime; and manages cooperation within international organisations such as the Collective Security Treaty Organization (CSTO), Commonwealth of Independent States (CIS) and SCO (Shanghai Cooperation Organisation). The GOU also participates in shaping the State Armament Programmes. Lieutenant General Sergey Rudskoy is the chief of the GOU and the first deputy chief of the General Staff since November 2015.

The **National Defence Management Centre** (Natsionalnyi tsentr upravleniya oboronoy, NTsUO), created by a Presidential Decree of 10 December 2013 and launched in December 2014, is a link between the General Staff and the troops; earlier it was the Central Command Post of the General Staff. The NTsUO chief is Colonel General Mikhail Mizintsev (since 2014). The NTsUO also incorporates the **4th Airborne Control Post of the Armed Forces of the Russian Federation** (Vozdushnyi punkt upravleniya Vooruzhonnymi silami RF; VzPU VS RF) equipped with Il-80 airborne command post aircraft based at Chkalovsky – operationally, these aircraft are subordinated to the 1338 Test Centre of the 929th State Flight-Test Centre (929 GLITs). Colonel Sergey Glazunov is the commander of the VzPU VS RF.

Functional division of the Russian Armed Forces

Russia's armed forces are composed of three **military branches** (vid vooruzhonnykh sil):

- Ground Troops (Sukhoputnyje voyska, SV)
- Aerospace Forces (Vozdushno-kosmicheskiye sily, VKS)
- Navy (Voyenno-morskoy flot, VMF)

and two **independent corps** (otdelnyi rod voysk):

- Strategic Rocket Troops (Raketnye voyska strategicheskogo naznacheniya, RVSN)
- Airborne Troops (Vozdushno-desantnye voyska, VDV)

as well as special troops (railway, road troops, health service, topographical service), rear-echelon units and other formations not belonging to the aforementioned branches.

In the past, each of the military branches and independent corps had its own air units, but they were gradually transferred to the Air Force. In 2003 the Air Force took over army aviation assets from the Ground Troops, and in 2011 – the aircraft from the RVSN and VDV. Currently, within the Russian Armed Forces, only the Aerospace Forces and the Navy have aviation assets. During a meeting with foreign military attachés in November 2018, the deputy commander of the VDV, Lieutenant General Alexander Vyaznikov revealed that in the future the VDV would be reinforced with 'army aviation subunits', which may be evidence of plans of to hand over flights or squadrons of helicopters to the VDV; for the time being these are only theoretical.

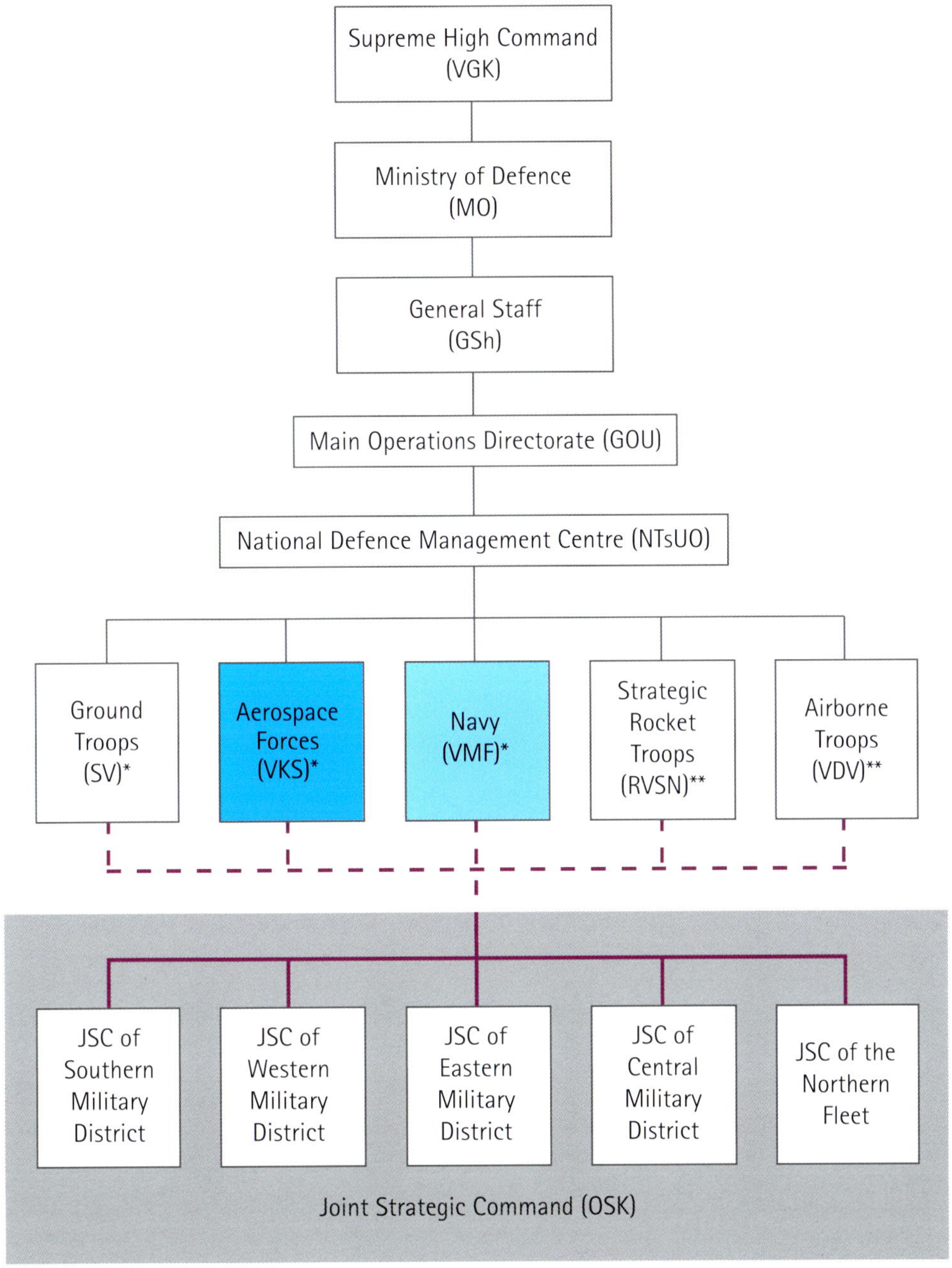

* military branch
** independent corps

Diagram showing the functional as well as territorial structure of the Russian armed forces.

– – – Forces supplied by Troops to the relevant military districts
(Harpia Publishing)

Other military organisations in Russia that operate aviation equipment but are not subordinated to the Ministry of Defence are the Federal National Guard Service (Rosgvardia), Federal Security Service (FSB) and Federal Guard Service (FSO).

Territorial division of the Russian Armed Forces

Territorially, the Russian Armed Forces are divided into five areas. Four are **military districts**, MD (Voyennyi Okrug, VO):

- Southern MD with HQ at Rostov-on-Don
- Western MD with HQ at St Petersburg
- Eastern MD with HQ at Khabarovsk
- Central MD with HQ at Yekaterinburg

The fifth area, detached on 15 December 2014, is the Northern Fleet with its HQ in Severomorsk, which received the status of military district. In future the creation of a sixth area on the basis of the Pacific Fleet is expected (currently this fleet is subordinated to the Eastern MD).

In 2010 a new body, the **Joint Strategic Command**, JSC (Obyedinyonnoye Strategicheskoye Komandovaniye, OSK) appeared in the command structure of the Russian Armed Forces. Currently there are five JSCs and each manages the military assets in its respective military district (or the Northern Fleet).

The formal name of the new structure is Joint Strategic Command of the Southern/Western/Eastern/Central Military District, or JSC of the Northern Fleet. Compared to the previous military districts (existing until 2010) that were primarily land force commands, the new JSCs have control over all general-purpose forces in their territories in times of peace and war.

Military District HQ

I St Petersburg (Western MD)

II Rostov-on-Don (Southern MD)

III Yekaterinburg (Central MD)

IV Khabarovsk (Eastern MD)

V Severomorsk (Northern Fleet)

Key

Military District HQ

Naval Aviation HQ

occupied territory

A map showing the current five Russian Military Districts. (Map by James Lawrence)

AEROSPACE FORCES

Vozdushno-Kosmicheskiye Sily, VKS
HQ: Moscow
Commander-in-chief: Colonel General Sergey Surovikin (since 22 November 2017)
Manpower: 165,000 people

The Aerospace Forces are commanded by the **Main Command of the Aerospace Forces** (Glavnoye Komandovaniye Vozdushno-Kosmicheskikh Sil, GK VKS), situated at Znamyenka street in Moscow.

For everyday management of the VKS, the **Commander-in-Chief Executive** (Upravleniye Glavnokomanduyushchego) and the **Main Staff of the Aerospace Forces** (Glavnyi Shtab VKS) were established within the GK VKS. The commander-in-chief of the VKS is Colonel General Sergey Surovikin. His first deputy and chief of staff is Lieutenant General Pavel Kurachenko.

The link between the Main Command and the subordinated troops is the **1073rd Management Centre of the Aerospace Forces** (Tsentr Upravleniya VKS).

The Aerospace Forces are composed of three corps, special duty units (electronic warfare, communications and automated control systems, engineering, meteorological), military units of technical and logistic support, guards, as well as military schools and research establishments.

These three **corps** (rod voysk) within the Aerospace Forces are as follows.

The **Air Force** (Voyenno-vozdushnye sily, VVS) is the operator of all fixed-wing aircraft and helicopters within the VKS. The Air Force's tasks are air protection of the country's most important sites; defeat of enemy ground troops and important objects; as well as air support of other military branches and corps. The commanding officer of the Air Force and the deputy commander-in-chief of the Aerospace Forces is Lieutenant General Andrey Yudin.

The **Air and Missile Defence Troops** (Voyska protivovozdushnoy i protivoraketnoy oborony, V PVO PRO) is tasked with protection of state and military command sites, groups of troops (forces), administrative and political centres, industrial regions, and the most important objects of the country's infrastructure against air and space attack. A part of the V PVO PRO is the 1st Army of Air and Missile Defence of Moscow with 53T6 (ABM-3 'Gazelle') anti-ballistic missiles and target detection systems. The 1st Army is directly subordinated to the GK VKS. The remaining assets of the V PVO PRO, i.e. air defence divisions with S-300PM1/PM2 (SA-20 'Gargoyle'), S-400 (SA-21 'Growler') and 96K6 Pantsir-S (SA-22 'Greyhound') surface-to-air missiles (SAMs), radio-technical troops and others are divided between the military districts. The commanding officer of the Air and Missile Defence Troops and the deputy commander-in-chief of the Aerospace Forces is Lieutenant General Viktor Gumyonnyi.

The **Space Troops** (Kosmicheskiye voyska, KV) have the mission of maintaining the ballistic missile early warning system, conducting space launches and surveillance and identification of space objects.. They control the 15th Army of Aerospace Forces (Special Purpose), the 820th Main Missile Attack Warning Centre, the 821st Main Space Intelligence Centre, the 1st State Test Cosmodrome Plesetsk, plus scientific and test facilities. The Space Troops are not subordinated to military districts, but directly to the GK VKS in Moscow. The commanding officer of the Space Troops and the deputy commander-in-chief of the Aerospace Forces is Lieutenant General Alexander Golovko.

Territorial division

Apart from the division of the Russian Aerospace Forces by equipment (aircraft in the Air Force, SAMs and radars within the Air and Missile Defence Troops, satellites within the Space Forces), the Aerospace Forces are also divided territorially, in common with the entire Russian Armed Forces. All aviation and air defence assets stationed within a military district are grouped within (and managed by) an **Air Force and Air Defence Army** (A VVS PVO):

- 4 A VVS PVO in Southern Military District
- 6 A VVS PVO in Western Military District
- 11 A VVS PVO in Eastern Military District
- 14 A VVS PVO in Central Military District

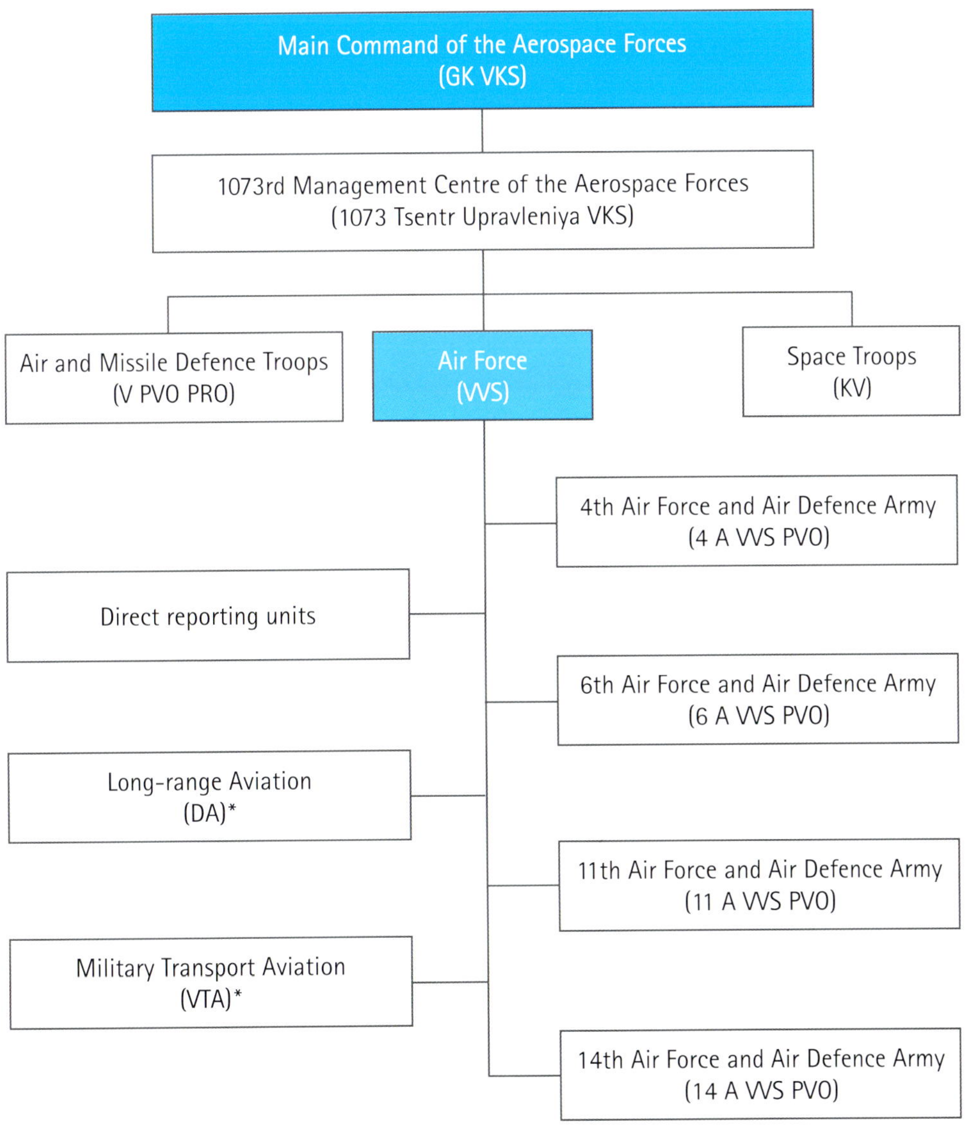

The structure of the Russian Aerospace Forces.

* DA and VTA are operationally subordinated to the Supreme High Command (VGK).

(Harpia Publishing)

One more army, the 45 A VVS PVO, is part of the Northern Fleet and is described in separately (see page 92).

Within the Aerospace Forces are two further commands established according to functional principle, operating across the territory of Russia and operationally subordinated to the Supreme High Command of the Russian Armed Forces:

- **Long-Range Aviation Command** is tasked with long-range bombardment of strategic targets with conventional or nuclear weapons,
- **Military Transport Aviation Command** is the main provider of airlift for Russian troops and equipment.

Apart from the units in the long-range and transport commands, plus tactical armies, there are also units subordinated directly to the Main Command of Aerospace Forces – so-called direct reporting units. These comprise scientific and research centres, training centres, a division of special duty aircraft in Chkalovsky and others.

Direct reporting units

A special place among the direct reporting units is taken by the 8th Aviation Division based at Chkalovsky airfield near Moscow, serving the Ministry of Defence and military branch commands, as well as the Russian air contingent deployed to Hmeimim air base in Syria since September 2015. Other direct reporting units described here include the aviation-related research organisations of the Russian MoD, evaluation and crew conversion centres, aviation academies and training units.

8th Aviation Division of Special Purpose (8 ADON)

HQ: Chkalovsky (Shcholkovo)
Commanding officer: Colonel Sergey Movchan

This division has its origins in a special aviation detachment formed in 1927 at Khodynka airfield in Moscow; since 1960 it has been stationed at Chkalovsky airfield in Shcholkovo. In 2009 it was transformed into the 6991 AvB and, in 2010, into the

Tu-154M RA-85155 is operated by the 223rd Flight Detachment based at Chkalovsky. (Piotr Butowski)

800 AvB. In early 2017 the traditional name 8 ADON was restored. Regardless of the reforms and name changes, it has always been tasked with serving armed forces commanders, as well as state authorities in wartime. (In peacetime, in contrast with many other nations, the president of Russia and members of the highest authorities are not transported by military aircraft but by the Special Flight Detachment Russia, or Spetsialnyi Lyotnyi Otryad Rossiya). The division also transports military personnel, special forces and others. Since 2015 the aircraft of 8 ADON have transported most of the military personnel to Syria and act as 'leaders' for groups of combat aircraft bound for Syria (not equipped with civilian transponders). At the peak of activities, they flew several dozens of missions to Syria each month.

The division's main equipment comprises passenger and transport aircraft, including around 20 each of the Tu-134 and Tu-154, around 10 each of the An-12, An-26, An-72, An-148, Il-76, Il-62 and Mi-8, plus single examples of the An-140, Il-96-400 and Tu-214; in total, more than 100 fixed-wing aircraft and helicopters are based at Chkalovsky. The airfield has a main runway 3,200m (10,499ft) long and 100m (328ft) wide and parallel emergency runway 3,630m (11,909ft) long and 70m (230ft) wide.

In addition, the Il-76MD-K, L-39 and Tu-204 aircraft of the Yuri Gagarin Cosmonaut Training Centre are based at Chkalovsky. Until 2009 this was a military unit; now it is a civil institution.

Unknown Composite Aviation Regiment (Special Purpose) [SAP(ON)]
HQ: Hmeimim, Syria

The entire Russian forces in Syria are organised within the Gruppirovka Voysk Vooruzhonnykh Sil Rossiyskoy Federatsii v Siriyskoy Arabskoy Respublike (Troops Group of the Armed Forces of the Russian Federation in Syrian Arab Republic). The air contingent, based at Hmeimim air base since September 2015, is an unknown composite aviation regiment (special purpose) that comprises bomber, fighter and helicopter squadrons. Additionally, there are a few Il-20 and An-30 reconnaissance aircraft as well as Forpost and Orlan-10 unmanned aerial vehicles (UAVs). Apart from the air units, S-400, Buk, Tor and Pantsir-S SAMs, as well as auxiliary units, are based at Hmeimim.

The Hmeimim base has been established on the perimeter of Bassel al-Assad International Airport, 20km (2 miles) southeast of the city of Latakia. New infrastructure was established by the Russians including an air traffic control tower, accommodation for the staff, taxiways, fuel stations and storage facilities. The airfield has two parallel runways 2,800m (9,186ft) long. The Russian air contingent has also periodically used Syrian Air Force bases at Shayrat and Tiyas (T-4), mostly for helicopters.

Bottom: A Su-30SM takes off from its Syrian base in September 2017, carrying an air defence armament for a combat air patrol. (MO RF).

Below: A pair of Su-25s from the unknown composite aviation regiment (special purpose) based at Hmeimim. (MoD RF).

A detailed ORBAT table of all direct reporting units can be found on page 51.

Research institutions

The research organisation serving the Russian military aviation is the **Central Research Institute of the Air Force of Ministry of Defence of Russian Federation** (Tsentralnyi Nauchno-Issledovatelskiy Institut Voyenno-Vozdushnikh Sil MO RF, TsNII VVS MO RF) at Shcholkovo, which in its current form was established in 2014 from several research institutes with long traditions. The head of the TsNII VVS is Alexander Palatnikov. The institute comprises the following research centres (Nauchno-Issledovatelskiy Tsentr; NITs):

The **Research Centre of Aviation Engineering and Armament** (NITs Aviatsionnoy Tekhniki i Voorozheniya, NITs AT V) in Shcholkovo defines the place and role of military aviation within the armed forces, assesses the needs of the air force in terms of new technology and specifies requirements for new fixed-wing aircraft, helicopters and their armament. The institute was established on 16 March 1960 as the 30 TsNII VVS and until now is commonly referred to as 'thirty'. For years the institute had a subsidiary at Noginsk near Moscow, specialised in automatic air force command and control systems; in December 2015 this element was moved to Shcholkovo as the centre's 4th Research Department (4 NIU).

The **Research Centre of Aircraft Operation and Overhaul** (NITs Ekspluatatsii i Remonta Aviatsionnoy Tekhniki, NITs ERAT, the former 13 GNII ERAT MO RF) at Lyubertsy near Moscow specialises in aircraft technical condition assessment, develops instructions for operation and overhauls and investigates air accidents. In 2012 the **Air Accident Investigation Centre** (Tsentr Obespecheniya Rassledovaniy Aviatsionnykh Proisshestviy, TsORAP) was established at Shcholkovo and this conducts both its own research and joint work with the NITs in Lyubertsy.

The **Research Test Centre of Aviation and Space Medicine and Military Ergonomics** (Nauchno-Issledovatelskiy Ispytatelnyi Tsentr Aviatsionno-Kosmicheskoy Meditsiny i Voyennoy Ergonomiki, NIITs AKM VE) was established in 1935 and is a leading research organisation for the study of the human factor in aviation.

Until 2010 the aforementioned research centres were independent institutes. In December 2010 they were incorporated into the 4 TsNII MO RF and then in April 2014 they were detached from the 4 TsNII and merged into the new TsNII VVS.

Aviation issues are also the responsibility of other military research institutes. The **Central Research Institute of Aerospace Defence Troops** (the former 2 TsNII MO RF) in Tver specialises in the theoretical problems of air and missile defence, including stealth characteristics of aircraft and airborne weapons.

The **Main Research Test Centre of Robotics** (Glavnyi Nauchno-Issledovatelskiy Ispytatelnyi Tsentr Robototekhniki, GNIITs RT MO RF), established in November 2012, specializes, among others, in scientific research on UAVs.

929th State Flight-Test Centre of Ministry of Defence of the Russian Federation (929 GLITs MO RF)

HQ: Akhtubinsk
Commanding officer: Major General Radik Bariyev (since 2009)

This institution conducts state evaluation of military aircraft, assessing the compliance of their characteristics with the requirements, which is the basis upon which an aircraft (weapon type) is commissioned into VKS service. The centre was established on 21 September 1920 at Khodynka airfield in Moscow.

The centre has a series of proving grounds in the Astrakhan district and further afield in the territory of neighbouring Kazakhstan, as well as proving grounds on the Black Sea coast (Feodosia) and in Kabardino-Balkaria (Nalchik). A component of the

MiG-31K RF-95217 '92 Red' on strength with the 929 GLITs at Akhtubinsk. This is one of the aircraft converted to carry the Kinzhal strike weapon, a version of the land-based Iskander ballistic missile.
(Piotr Butowski)

929 GLITs is the **267th(?) Test Pilot Training Centre** (Tsentr Podgotovki Lyotchikov Ispytateley).

The base of the 929 GLITs consists of two joint airfields, but the smaller one is used only as a parking area. The main runway is 4,000m (13,123ft) long and 60m (197ft) wide; the dimensions of the parallel reserve runways are 2,500 by 500m (8,202 by 1,640ft). There are always several examples of new aircraft types undergoing evaluation at Akhtubinsk. For instance, according to satellite photographs of 6 September 2018 there were two Su-57, five Su-35, seven Su-34 and four Su-30SM fighters at the base, as well as 18 MiG-31s, about half of which were MiG-31Ks.

The 929th Centre's headquarters and main research departments (Nauchno-Issledovatelskoye Upravleniye; NIU) are based at Akhtubinsk, but the centre also has several test centres based elsewhere:

The **4th Research Department** (4 NIU), specialised in aircraft engines, is based at Chkalovsky. The same base also houses a test centre (unknown number) conducting state evaluation of helicopters, basic trainers and transport aircraft.

The **Test Centre (Naval)**, conducting evaluation of naval fixed-wing aircraft and helicopters as well as naval weaponry, is based at Feodosia, Crimea. Between 1992 and 2014 the Feodosia centre belonged to the Ukrainian Air Force, but sporadically fulfilled Russian orders. After the annexation of Crimea by Russia, the centre became a part of the 929 GLITs in December 2014.

The **Mountain Research Test Centre of Aviation Engineering and Weapon**, where aircraft and weapons are tested in high mountain conditions, is based at Nalchik in the Caucasus foothills. The centre maintains its own **386th(?) Aviation Test Squadron** at the local airfield, and a proving ground.

The **13th Aerostatic Test Centre** in Volsk near Saratov specialises in testing balloons and airships. The commander as of 2017 was Colonel Valery Pelle.

Su-35S RF-95242 '03 Red' belongs to the Lipetsk-based 968th Research Instructor Composite Aviation Regiment. The unit began to accept the first deliveries of the new fighter in 2014. (Piotr Butowski)

The **395th (?) Test Aviation Squadron** is located at Bagay-Baranovka airfield in the vicinity of Volsk, operating An-26, An-72 and Mi-8 aircraft.

The **1338th Test Centre** at Chkalovsky operates Il-80 airborne command post and Il-82 communications relay aircraft serving the 4th Airborne Control Post of the Armed Forces of the Russian Federation.

The 929 GLITs also maintains outposts at Znamyensk (Kapustin Yar), 50km (31 miles) northwest of Akhtubinsk, and at Klyuchi airfield on Kamchatka, 6,900km (4,287 miles) away from Akhtubinsk.

4th State Air Personnel Preparation and Military Evaluation Centre of Ministry of Defence of the Russian Federation (4 GTs PAP VI MO RF)

HQ: Lipetsk

Commanding officer: Lieutenant General Yuri Sushkov

The centre is tasked with conducting military evaluation of initial batches of tactical combat aircraft, developing air force tactics and training pilots in combat application of the aircraft. The centre has departments specialised in fighter, attack and bomber (tactical) aircraft, as well as air traffic control, mathematical modelling, aerodynamics and combat application. The centre's specialists work out aircraft combat application instructions for pilots of operational units.

During 2010–11, the remaining combat training centres – responsible for the army aviation at Torzhok, transport aviation at Ivanovo, long-range aviation at Ryazan and unmanned aircraft at Kolomna – were subordinated to the Lipetsk centre. It did not last long and after a couple of years their independence was restored.

Equipped with twin-seat Su-30SM fighters, the Russkiye Vityazi aerobatic team is home-based at Kubinka, where it is one of two such units assigned to the 237th Aviation Technology Demonstration Centre.
(Piotr Butowski)

The 4th Centre currently comprises the 968th Regiment at Lipetsk, a fighter squadron at Savasleyka and the 237th Demonstration Centre at Kubinka. The Lipetsk centre has also two training areas: Ratchino near Voronezh and Pogonovo near Lipetsk. The centre was decorated with Lenin and Red Banner Orders and bears the name of Valery Chkalov.

968th Research Instructor Composite Aviation Regiment (968 IISAP)
Location: Lipetsk
Commanding officer: Colonel Sergey Aksyonov

This regiment is responsible for receiving deliveries of the first batches of new tactical aircraft. For instance, the regiment received the first Su-34 in 2007, Yak-130 in 2010, Su-30SM in 2013, Su-35S in 2014 and was due to receive the first Su-57 in 2019. Currently the regiment has four squadrons of Sukhoi fighters (Su-27, Su-30SM and Su-35S), Mikoyan fighters (MiG-29), tactical bombers (Su-24 and Su-34) and attack aircraft (Su-25), as well as a detachment of An-26 transport aircraft.

The regiment includes also the Russkiye Sokoly (Russian Hawks) aerobatic team flying Su-35S fighters. The regiment bears the title Sevastopol and is decorated with the Red Banner and Suvorov orders.

The Lipetsk airfield has two runways: the main runway is 3,000m (9,843ft) long and 60m (197ft) wide. The second, shorter runway has been out of use for many years and is now used to park preserved aircraft: these comprise more than 50 MiG-29s, several dozen MiG-31s, a dozen Su-27s and single aircraft of other types.

This upgraded MiG-31BM, RF-92380 '92 Blue', is operated by an unknown aviation squadron based at Savasleyka. (Piotr Butowski)

Unknown Independent Aviation Squadron (OAE)
Location: Savasleyka
Commanding officer: Lieutenant Colonel Aleksander Pavlushkin

This squadron operates MiG-31 interceptors, and has been equipped with the MiG-31BM version since 2008. The runway at Savasleyka is 2,700m 8,858(ft) long and 50m (164ft) wide.

237th Aviation Technology Demonstration Centre (237 TsPAT)
Location: Kubinka
Commanding officer: Colonel Andrey Alekseyev

This is one of the most elite units within the Russian Aerospace Forces. Since 27 April 2009, it has been subordinated to the Lipetsk centre. The 237th TsPAT hosts two aerobatics teams: the Russkiye Vityazi (Russian Knights) created in April 1991 with Su-30SMs (Su-27s until 2016), and the Strizhi (Swifts) created in May 1991 with MiG-29 fighters. Kubinka is also home to An-30 aircraft participating in the Treaty on Open Skies programme. The Il-20M reconnaissance aircraft shot down over Syria on 17 September 2018 was also from Kubinka. The airfield has a runway 2,500m (8,202ft) long and 80m (262ft) wide. Aircraft demonstrations for the Russian authorities and foreign delegations often take place at Kubinka, as well as the aviation element of the International Military-Technical Forum 'Army'. The 237 TsPAT bears the Guard and Proskurovsky titles, has been awarded with the Kutuzov and Alexander Nevsky orders and also carries the name of Air Marshal Ivan Kozhedub. The regiment day is 22 March.

344th State Combat Training and Flight Crew Conversion Centre of Army Aviation (344 GTsBP PLS AA)

HQ: Torzhok
Commanding officer: Colonel Sergey Baunov

The 344th Centre is tasked with conducting military evaluation of helicopters and conversion of pilots to new types. Torzhok always receives new helicopters first; it has operated the Mi-28N since 2008, Ka-52 since 2010 and Mi-35M since 2011. Since 12 April 1992, the centre has included the Berkuty (Eagles) aerobatics team flying Mi-28N helicopters (Mi-24s until 2011). The helicopters of the 344th Centre are grouped within two research-instructor units. Most are assigned to the **696th Research Instructor Helicopter Regiment** (696 IIVP) at Torzhok, while several Mi-8s and Mi-24s are operated by the **92nd Research Instructor Helicopter Squadron** (92 IIVE) at Klin airfield, 130km (81 miles) away from Torzhok, towards Moscow.

924th State Unmanned Aviation Centre of Ministry of Defence of the Russian Federation (924 GTs BpA MO RF)

HQ: Kolomna
Commanding officer: Colonel Alexey Fedorko

The main task of the 924 GTs BpA is conducting military evaluation of unmanned aerial vehicles (UAVs), developing tactics for their use and training the specialists that operate these systems. The Russian Aerospace Forces operate only a small portion of these; most of the approximately 2,000 military UAVs in Russia are smaller systems issued to the Ground Troops.

According to an official release, 'specialists of the centre conducted air reconnaissance and ensured safety during the Winter Olympic Games in Sochi [in 2014], took part in annual exercises at various levels, carried out special tasks [military actions] in the Southern Military District [eastern Ukraine], the Republic of Crimea and Tajikistan.' Sub-units of the 924 GTs BpA also operate UAVs in Syria.

Mi-28N RF-92130 '12 Yellow' is part of the Torzhok-based 344th State Combat Training and Flight Crew Conversion Centre of Army Aviation. (Piotr Butowski)

Mi-8AMTSh RF-91209, Bort '51', is operated by the 92nd Research Instructor Helicopter Squadron at Klin airfield. The unit is one of two research-instructor units assigned to the 344th Centre. (Piotr Butowski)

185th Combat Training and Combat Application Centre of the Aerospace Forces (185 TsBP BPr VKS)

HQ: Astrakhan
Commanding officer: Colonel Aleksey Rot'ko

This is the only such formation in Russia tasked with providing realistic combat tactics training for fighters (and for air defence) from other units. The unit is tasked with replicating combat conditions, including large-scale interaction with aircraft, air defences and radio-technical assets of the 'enemy'. These 'enemies' are the units of the 185th Centre – sometimes referred to as the 'Russian Aggressor Squadron'.

The air component of the 185 TsBP BPr is the 116th Fighter Centre based at Privolzhsky, a few kilometres away from Astrakhan. In addition to this, the 185th Centre is responsible for the 67th Firing Range Ashuluk (Tambovka), 130km (81 miles) north of

These MiG-29SMT fighters, '21 Blue' and '23 Blue', belong to the 116th Combat Application Training Centre of Fighter Aviation at Privolzhsky – the 'Russian Aggressor Squadron'. (Piotr Butowski)

The Air Force Academy's 221st Training Aviation Base at Shagol airfield in Chelyabinsk is equipped with Tu-134Sh (RF-66031, '36 Red' seen here) and An-26Sh aircraft for navigator training. (Piotr Butowski)

Astrakhan, as well as other units at Ashuluk: the 42nd Surface-to-Air Missiles Training Centre, radar and radio units, launch sites and control stations for aerial target, and others. Two other training areas, Mukhor-Konduy and Telemba near Chita (4,600km, 2,858 miles away from Astrakhan) are also subordinated to the 185th Centre.

116th Combat Application Training Centre of Fighter Aviation (116 UTsBPr IA)
Location: Privolzhsky (Astrakhan)

This unit has operated MiG-29s since 1989, and the latest MiG-29SMT variant since 2016. Currently there are more than 40 MiG-29s at the base, but only around half of these are active. The pilots of the centre pride themselves on having the highest flying time in the entire tactical aviation in Russia, exceeding 120 hours per year. In December 2012 a major refurbishment of Privolzhsky air base began. One of the two runways was lengthened from 2,500m to 3,500m (8,202ft to 11,483ft) and widened from 42m to 60m (138ft to 197ft); the other one remained unchanged. The main portion of the work was finished in 2015, but some parking places, communication roads and other infrastructure still needed to be completed.

A detailed ORBAT table of all research institutions can be found on page 51.

Military aviation education

Air Force Military Educational and Scientific Centre 'Air Force Academy named after Professor N. E. Zhukovsky and Y. A. Gagarin' (VUNTs VVS VVA)

HQ: Voronezh
Commanding officer: Colonel General Gennady Zibrov

The Syzran branch of the Air Force Academy provides tuition to army aviation pilots and technical specialists. Its equipment includes Ka-226V RF-13350, '416 Yellow'. (Piotr Butowski)

The Air Force Academy trains pilots and navigators, plus technical and auxiliary personnel, for Russian military aviation. It also educates command staff: each officer occupying the post of regiment commander or above must graduate from a command studies course at the Air Force Academy. In total, 12,000 people study at the academy at any given time.

The current Zhukovsky and Gagarin Air Force Academy was established in April 2012 through the merger of several other academies: the Zhukovsky Air Force Engineering Academy in Moscow, the Gagarin Air Force Academy in Monino and the Mili-

Yak-130 RF-44579 '64 Red' is operated by the 209 UAvB of the Krasnodar Military Aviation College of Pilots and is based at Borisoglebsk. (Piotr Butowski)

L-410UVP-E3 RF-94625 '48 Red' from the 217 UAvB at Rtishchevo. (Piotr Butowski)

tary Aviation Engineering University in Voronezh; the resulting institution is located in Voronezh. Previously, in 2009, smaller military flying schools from Irkutsk, Stavropol and Tambov were also moved to Voronezh. Later, in 2012–13, a further two aviation schools, in Chelyabinsk and Syzran, were transformed into branches of the academy (without changing location). In 2018 it was planned to restore the independence of the Chelyabinsk and Syzran branches, but this does not appear to have taken place.

The **Chelyabinsk branch of the Air Force Academy** (dating back to 1936) trains air navigators, forward air controllers and air traffic controllers. The branch has its own **221st Training Aviation Base** at Shagol airfield in Chelyabinsk with Tu-134Sh and An-26Sh aircraft for navigator training.

The **Syzran branch of the Air Force Academy** (dating back to 1940) trains pilots and technical specialists of army aviation (helicopters). The branch has a subordinated **339th Training Aviation Base** with two airfields, Syzran (Mi-8 and Mi-24) and Sokolovyi near Saratov (Ansat, Ka-226 and Mi-2), as well as a duty post at Pugachev airfield, used periodically.

Krasnodar Military Aviation College of Pilots (KVVAUL)

HQ: Krasnodar
Commanding officer: Major General Oleg Makovetsky

This is the only college providing a syllabus for military fixed-wing pilots in Russia (helicopter pilots are trained at Syzran). Since 2009 it has gradually absorbed the other remaining schools. The college traces its history back to a flying school established in Chita in 1938; it bears the name of Hero of the Soviet Union A. K. Serov. During 2010–15 the Krasnodar college was a branch of the Air Force Academy; it regained independence on 1 August 2015. In 2018 a total of 350 pilots graduated from the Krasnodar college; a similar number is planned for the following years.

General military and theoretical teaching is conducted in Krasnodar. Specialised faculties are located in Armavir (fighter aviation), Borisoglebsk (tactical bomber and attack aviation) and Balashov (transport and long-range bomber aviation). The school has nine bases equipped with training aircraft.

A detailed ORBAT table of all military training units can be found on page 51.

Military pilots training

The pilot schools in Krasnodar (fixed-wing aircraft) and Syzran (helicopters) accept candidates with a secondary education, aged 16-22 (completing military service to the age of 24, or 27 when in contract service). Previous elementary flight training on light aircraft – for instance in a flying club – is desired, but not necessary.

Studies take five years. The first two years comprise general military and theoretical indoctrination. Flying begins in the third year with sorties alongside an instructor in Yak-130 and L-39C jet aircraft (or, for rotary-wing pilots, Ansat-U, Ka-226V and Mi-2 helicopters). The candidates gain basic flying skills in daytime visual meteorological conditions, first practicing take-offs and landings. After several dozen short (usually 15-30 minutes) sorties with an instructor, the trainee makes their first solo flight. Next come the basics of instrument flying, including instrument landing approaches, basics of navigation and flying with a map. Emergency situation procedures, including engine failures and stalls, are also practiced. At the end of this stage of training the trainees conduct their first sorties in a two-ship formation and a night flight.

In the fourth year, pilots are divided into fighter (further training in Armavir), tactical bomber and attack aircraft (Borisoglebsk), or transport and long-range bomber aircraft (Balashov, Rtishchevo) streams. The basics of combat application are added at this stage in the training. Flights are made at increasingly higher speeds and with higher G-loads; future helicopter pilots convert to the 'heavy' Mi-8 and Mi-24. Individual mission elements are brought together in increasingly complex scenarios. Instrument, formation and low-altitude flights are now made more often. Finally, elements of air combat tactics are added, inckuding 'chasing the tail' of another manoeuvring aircraft and sorties in four-ship formations.

The fifth year comprises advanced and combat training, during which the future pilot becomes acquainted with the next elements of aviation tactics and with combat aircraft. Training is conducted on the MiG-29, Su-25 and Su-27 (or the L-410 or An-26 for future multi-engine aircraft pilots). Students of the helicopter flying school now practice training on Mi-8 helicopters in operational units.

Average flying time of a graduate amounts to around 150–160 hours, including 15-20 hours on combat aircraft. The graduate is promoted to the rank of first officer and receives a technical college degree.

Long-Range Aviation

Dalnyaya aviatsiya (DA)

HQ: Moscow
Commanding officer: Lieutenant General Sergey Kobylash

The Long-Range Aviation (Dalnyaya Aviatsiya, DA) is the heavy bomber force operationally subordinated to the Supreme High Command of the Russian Armed Forces and managed by **Long-Range Aviation Command** of the Aerospace Forces.

The DA is tasked with bombardment of strategic targets with nuclear or conventional air-launched cruise missiles (ALCMs) or bombs. The first combat operation for Russian strategic bombers was the bombing of Syria on 17 November 2015, when Tu-160 and Tu-95MS bombers launched Kh-101 and Kh-555 cruise missiles.

The DA has two almost symmetrical air divisions, the 22 TBAD at Engels air base in Europe and the 326 TBAD at Ukrainka air base in Far East. Each division has a regiment of strategic bombers and one or two regiments of long-range bombers; in Russian nomenclature there is a distinct differentiation between Tu-95MS or Tu-160 'strategic bombers' and the Tu-22M3 'long-range bomber'. Long-range Aviation celebrates its day on 23 December; Czar Nicholas II approved the decision to create the first squadron of Ilya Muromets heavy bombers on that day in 1914.

Power projection

Strategic bombers with nuclear missiles have double importance for Russia. Firstly, Russia considers 'nuclear deterrent' to be single guarantee of its security. In this view, without possessing (nuclear) strategic weapons, Russia would be immediately attacked by NATO, led by the US, and deprived of its oil and gas.

Secondly, Russia periodically deploys its heavy bombers to conduct out-of-area operations as a power-projection tool. These operations have included activity in the Pacific, near Japan, Alaska and the coast of Canada and, at the opposite end of the globe – along the coast of Norway and the United Kingdom, Denmark and Iceland. The most 'exotic' recent international visits by Russian strategic bombers were those of two Tu-95MS bombers from Ukrainka to Indonesia in December 2017, and two Tu-160 bombers from Engels to Venezuela in December 2018 (previously, Tu-160s visited Venezuela in 2008 and 2013).

22nd Heavy Bomber Aviation Division (22 TBAD)

HQ: Engels
Commanding officer: Colonel Oleg Pchela

This division was formed in March 1942. In 2010 it was transformed into the 6950 AvB and in 2015 it was reorganised as the 22 TBAD. The division bears the titles Guard and Donbass; it is decorated with the Red Banner order.

Tu-160 strategic bombers are operated exclusively by the 121st Heavy Bomber Aviation Regiment at Engels in European Russia. This is Tu-160 RF-94115 '08 Red', named *Vitaliy Kopylov.* (Fydor Borisov)

121st Heavy Bomber Aviation Regiment (121 TBAP)
Location: Engels
Commanding officer: Colonel Alexander Khabarov

This regiment's history dates back to 1940. Since 1992 it has operated Tu-160 bombers. In 2009, the 121st Regiment was transformed into an aviation group within the 6950 AvB. In 2015 the 121 TBAP was re-established with responsibility for all aircraft at Engels base: the Tu-160 bombers of the former 121st Regiment and Tu-95MS of the former 184th Regiment. The 184 TBAP had been formed at Engels on 1 September 2000 with Tu-95MS bombers redeployed from Mozdok base.

A pair of Tu-95MS bombers from the 121st Heavy Bomber Aviation Regiment during operations at a snowy Engels. (Piotr Butowski)

Tu-22M3 RF-94154 '24 Red' from the 52nd Heavy Bomber Aviation Regiment at Shaykovka. The aircraft is named *Mikhail Shidlovskiy*. (Piotr Butowski)

Currently the 121 TBAP has a squadron of Tu-160 bombers (16 aircraft) and a squadron of Tu-95MS bombers (around 15 aircraft). Engels air base was reconstructed during 2012–17. In parallel to the main runway, which is 3,500m (2,175ft) long and 70m (230ft) wide, a new runway of the same length and 60m (197ft) width was built. Subsequently the aircraft parking area was entirely reconstructed. The regimental day is 27 June.

52nd Heavy Bomber Aviation Regiment (52 TBAP)
Location: Shaykovka
Commanding officer: Colonel Alexander Shcherbinin

The 52 BAP was formed in 1944 and has been based at Shaykovka since 1959. It has been operating Tu-22M bombers since 1982. In 2009 the regiment was transformed into the 6951 AvB, then into an aviation group of the 6950 AvB and then back into the 52 TBAP. In 2010 the Tu-22M3 bombers from the disbanded 840 TBAP based at Soltsy were transferred to Shaykovka; currently, the 52 TBAP maintains a duty post at Soltsy air base, which is occasionally used. The Shaykovka air base has one runway 3,500m (2,175ft) long and 80m (262ft) wide; approximately 25 Tu-22M3s are stationed there. The regimental day is 4 October.

40th Composite Aviation Regiment (40 SAP)
Location: Vysokiy (Olenyegorsk)

Until 2010 this unit was known as the 924th Naval Missile Carrier Aviation Regiment. On 1 April 2011 it was subordinated to the Russian Air Force as an aviation group of the

Formerly assigned to the 568th Naval Aviation Regiment based at Mongokhto, Tu-22M3 RF-34083 '55 Red' is today part of the 200th Heavy Bomber Aviation Regiment at Belaya. (UAC)

6950 AvB, but remained at Olenyegorsk air base; since 2015 it has been known as the 40 SAP. For the time being the 40 SAP has no titles, but perhaps will inherit the titles (Guard and Kiev) and orders (Red Banner and Suvorov) of the 924th Regiment. Currently there are around 40 Tu-22M3 bombers at Olenyegorsk, but most are not in service; only one squadron is active. The regiment is identified as 'composite' because it also operates transport aircraft and helicopters (including the heavy Mi-26), serving the Arctic bases. Olenyegorsk has one runway 3,500m (2,175ft) long and 80m (262ft) wide.

326th Heavy Bomber Aviation Division (326 TBAD)

HQ: Ukrainka (Seryshevo)
Commanding officer: Colonel Sergey Kuvaldin

This division was formed on 10 October 1943. In 2009, it was transformed into the 6952 AvB; at the same time it received the Guard and Sevastopol-Berlin titles and the Red Banner order from one of its regiments, the 182 TBAP. In 2015 the base was transformed back into the 326 TBAD, retaining its titles. Currently the division comprises two regiments, based at Belaya and Ukrainka air bases, plus duty posts at Anadyr and Tiksi.

The fleet of the 27th Composite Aviation Regiment at Tambov includes these Tu-134UBLs. (Piotr Butowski)

A US Air Force F-22A Raptor intercepts a Tu-95MS off the coast of Alaska on 11 September 2018. Power projection is one of the key roles of the Russian heavy bomber fleet. (US DoD)

182nd Heavy Bomber Aviation Regiment (182 TBAP)
Location: Ukrainka (Seryshevo)
Commanding officer: Colonel Alexander Kokarev

Before the reform of 2009, two Tu-95MS bomber regiments, the 79 TBAP and 182 TBAP, were based at Ukrainka; in 2009 both were transformed into aviation groups of the 6952 AvB. In December 2015 only one regiment (182) was re-established and all aircraft were transferred to it. The 182 TBAP at Ukrainka currently has around 30 Tu-95MS bombers. Ukrainka air base has one runway 3,500m (2,175ft) long and 60m (197ft) wide.

200th Heavy Bomber Aviation Regiment (200 TBAP)
Location: Belaya
Commanding officer: Colonel Dmitry Pitreniyeks

This regiment was established in October 1943 and until 1994 was based in Belarus. In 2009 the regiment was transformed into the 6953 AvB and in 2010 it became an aviation group of the 6952 AvB. At the same time a squadron of Tu-22M3 aircraft from the disbanded 444 TBAP was moved to Belaya from nearby Vozdvizenka.

On 1 April 2011 another Tu-22M3 squadron, previously a part of the 568th Naval Aviation Regiment based at Mongokhto, was assigned to Belaya. In 2016 the previous 200 TBAP name was restored. The regiment has Guard and Brest titles, as well as the Red Banner order. The regimental day is 13 January. Belaya air base has one runway, 4,000m (13,123ft) long and 70m (230ft) wide.

Currently there are approximately 40 Tu-22M3 bombers at the base (it is unknown how many of these are airworthy). The regiment also comprises a detachment of An-30 photographic reconnaissance aircraft.

43rd Combat Application and Flight Crew Conversion Centre of Long-Range Aviation (43 TsBP PLS DA)

Location: Dyagilevo (Ryazan)
Commanding officer: Colonel Nikolay Varpakhovich

This centre was established in 1940 and has carried its current name since 1968. On 1 September 2010, the 43rd Centre was subordinated to the 4th Centre at Lipetsk, but in late 2013 it was returned to Long-range Aviation. The centre has a handful of Tu-22M3 bombers at its disposal, plus Tu-95MS strategic bombers at Ryazan, as well as training aircraft within the 27 SAP at Tambov. Dyagilevo air base in Ryazan has one runway 3,000m (9,843ft) long and 70m (230ft) wide.

The centre also maintains an aviation museum, the most interesting exhibits of which include Myasishchev M-4 and 3M-T as well as Tupolev Tu-95K-20 aircraft.

27th Composite Aviation Regiment (27 SAP)

Location: Tambov

Previously this was a bomber pilot school and training regiment, which in 1998 were subordinated to the 43rd Centre at Ryazan. The regiment currently has a squadron of Tu-134UBL trainers and a squadron of An-26 transport aircraft. Around 40 Tu-134s can be found at the airfield, but most of them are not in service. The runway at Tambov is 2,500m (8,202ft) long and 50m (164ft) wide.

An-26 RF-92950 '59 Red' is part of the training fleet within the 27th Composite Aviation Regiment at Tambov. (Piotr Butowski)

Il-78M RF-94290 '31 Blue' demonstrates aerial refuelling with a Tu-160. The 203rd Independent Aviation Regiment of Tanker Aircraft at Ryazan is the only Russian unit of its type. (Piotr Butowski)

203rd Independent Aviation Regiment of Tanker Aircraft (203 OAP SZ)

Location: Dyagilevo (Ryazan)

This tanker regiment was formed in 1960 at Engels with Myasishchev M-4-2 aircraft; since 1989 it has operated Il-78s. On 1 December 1994 the regiment assumed the number and traditions of the renowned 203 TBAP, and on 1 September 2000 was moved from Engels to Dyagilevo. During the years of turbulence between 2009–13 the regiment was first disbanded (its Il-78 aircraft were assigned to the 43rd Centre) and then in December 2013 it was re-established with the previous 203 OAP SZ name and Guard and Orel titles. This is the only tanker aircraft unit in Russia.

A detailed ORBAT table of all Long-range Aviation units can be found on page 52.

Forward airfields

Russian strategic bombers are based at Engels and Ukrainka, situated near the southern frontier of the country. For this reason, in order to hit a target in the north (for example in the United States, flying over the North Pole), forward airfields (aerodrom podskoka) are necessary. These are found at Anadyr, Tiksi and Vorkuta airfields in the far north of Russia, where duty posts (Aviatsyonnaya Komendatura, AvK) subordinated directly to the Long-Range Aviation Command are maintained, with few personnel, a limited supply of fuel and runway in satisfactory condition. When necessary, bombers arriving from the south of the country land at forward airfields, refuel and take-off to continue their mission.

A duty post is also maintained at Kamensk Uralsky (199 AvK), where aircraft flying from the European part of Russia to the Far East, or in the opposite direction, can make a refuelling stop; it is subordinated to the 43rd TsBP PLS at Ryazan.

In October 2017 a Tu-22M3 bomber (commanded by Colonel D. Golubinsky) from the 200 TBAP at Belaya made the type's first landing at Anadyr airfield on Chukotka, 700km (435 miles) from Alaska; it made stopovers at Ukrainka and Yelizovo. On 15 August 2018 a pair of Tu-160 bombers landed for the first time at Anadyr.

Military Transport Aviation

Voyenno-transportnaya aviatsiya (VTA)

HQ: Moscow
Commanding officer: Lieutenant General Vladimir Benediktov

Military Transport Aviation is the main provider of aerial lift for the Russian Armed Forces. It is operationally subordinated to the Supreme High Command of the Russian Armed Forces and managed by **Military Transport Aviation Command** of the Aerospace Forces.

Throughout its existence, the main task of the VTA has been serving the airborne forces, dropping troops and materiel by parachute or after landing. A second role is the support of military aviation deployments, i.e. transport of equipment, ground crews and others during a redeployment of aircraft to another base. Next is the transport of personnel and materiel from other military branches and corps.

The VTA has six VTAD regiments with 100 Il-76s supplemented by a small number of 'super heavy' An-124s and a few An-22s. As a result of the reforms of 2010, previously untypical units became part of the VTA: these include the A-50 early warning aircraft at Ivanovo and squadrons of An-2 aircraft used for parachute training by the Airborne Troops.

Four OTSAP regiments serving military districts' commands also formally belong to the VTA. In fact, these are managed by the commands of the respective VVS PVO armies, and are therefore described in their respective chapters.

The VTA day is 1 June, commemorating the formation of the first air-landing unit on that date in 1931.

12th Military Transport Aviation Division (12 VTAD)

HQ: Migalovo (Tver)
Commanding officer: Colonel Ruslan Fetkulin

This division was formed on 4 June 1943; since 1983 its HQ has been located in Tver. During 2009–15 it existed in the form of the 6955 AvB. The division has Guard and Mga (after the River Mga) titles and Red Banner order. The divisional day is 4 June.

196th Military Transport Aviation Regiment (196 VTAP)

Location: Migalovo (Tver)
Commanding officer: Colonel Leonid Rusin

This regiment's history dates back to 1943; after World War II it was based in Tartu, Estonia and in autumn 1992 was redeployed to Migalovo near Tver. Since 1980 the regiment has operated Il-76s. Migalovo air base has one runway 2,500m (8,202ft) long and 50m (164ft) wide.

Currently the regiment has around 20 Il-76s and a handful of An-22 aircraft. The regiment has Guard and Minsk titles; the regimental day is 25 May.

Now a rarity in Russian military service, the An-22 is flown by the 196th Military Transport Aviation Regiment at Tver. This is RA-09342. (Piotr Butowski)

334th Military Transport Aviation Regiment (334 VTAP)
Location: Kresty (Pskov)
Commanding officer: Colonel Andrey Pavlovsky

This regiment was formed on 1 June 1944; since 1948 it has been stationed at Kresty air base near Pskov; the runway's dimensions are 2,500m (8,202ft) by 50m (164ft). Since 1979 the regiment has operated Il-76s and now has around 20 in its inventory. The regiment has the title Berlin and the Red Banner order. The regimental day is 1 June.

566th Military Transport Aviation Regiment (566 VTAP)
Location: Seshcha (Bryansk)
Commanding officer: Colonel Alexander Kozhemyako

This is the only unit operating the world's heaviest transport aircraft, the An-124. The regiment was formed on 7 September 1941 and since May 1956 has been stationed at Seshcha. In 1970 it was equipped with what was then the world's largest transport aircraft, the An-22, exchanging this for the even larger An-124 in 1987. Seshcha air base has a unique layout. It has a runway 3,100m (10,171ft) long and 80m (262ft) wide that projects into half of the circular aircraft parking area. The regiment has the Solnechnegorsk title and Red Banner and Kutuzov 3rd Grade orders. The regimental day is 7 September.

18th Military Transport Aviation Division (18 VTAD)

HQ: Orenburg
Commanding officer: Colonel Dmitry Sukhoruchkin.

This is one of the youngest formations in the VKS. The division's HQ was established on 30 November 2017 in Orenburg and three regiments at Orenburg, Ulyanovsk and Taganrog were subordinated to it. The new division received the number and traditions of the 18 VTAD that existed during 1942–98, including the Guard and Taganrog titles, as well as Red Banner, Suvorov 2nd Grade and Kutuzov 2nd Grade orders. The divisional day is 23 October.

117th Military Transport Aviation Regiment (117 VTAP)

Location: Orenburg
Commanding officer: Colonel Dmitry Irushkin

This is one of the more interesting units in the Russian Aerospace Forces. It was formed on 1 July 1938 as a long-range bomber regiment; in 1959 it was transformed into a Tu-16 aerial tanker regiment and in 1969 it became the 117th Electronic Warfare Aircraft Regiment, equipped with An-12PP aircraft. Until 1994 the regiment was based in Lithuania. In November that year it moved to Orenburg in Russia and was re-equipped with Il-76MD transport aircraft, retaining one squadron of An-12PPS jamming aircraft. The unit survived the period 2009–14 as an aviation group within the 6955 AvB. In December 2014 the regiment was re-established as the 117 OVTAP, and after being assigned to the 18 VTAD lost the 'independent' designation. The regiment had the title Berlin and the Kutuzov Order 3rd Grade, but lost them during the transformation. The regimental day is 1 July. Orenburg air base has one runway 2,500m (8,202ft) long and 45m wide.

Airborne troops prepare to embark Il-76MD RF-76650 operated by the 334th Military Transport Aviation Regiment in Pskov, during a VDV excercise in July 2018. (Russian MoD)

A single Russian Aerospace Forces unit operates the huge An-124 transport. An-124-100 RF-82032 is assigned to the 556th Military Transport Aviation Regiment at Seshcha. (Piotr Butowski)

Currently the regiment has two transport squadrons with 20 Il-76MD aircraft and an electronic warfare squadron with three An-12PPS and three new Il-22PP Porubshchik aircraft. A squadron of An-2 aircraft (the former 340 OVTAE) subordinated to the 117th regiment is based in Omsk, 1,250km (776 miles) east of Orenburg. They are used for parachute training of soldiers of the 242nd Training Centre of Airborne Troops. The squadron has around 10 An-2s and a handful of An-26 and An-72 aircraft.

235th Military Transport Aviation Regiment (235 VTAP)

Location: Ulyanovsk Vostochnyi
Commanding officer: Colonel Vadim Dyrdin

Along with the establishment of the 18 VTAD on 1 December 2017 at Ulyanovsk Vostochnyi (East; this is also a factory airfield of the Aviastar-SP production facility), a new regiment, the 235 VTAP, was formed. Initially, a squadron of 10 Il-76MD aircraft, transferred from Orenburg's 117th Regiment, was assigned to the 235 VTAP; the precise movements are unclear, since the number of aircraft at Orenburg did not diminish and the total in Ulyanovsk did not increase. The squadron of An-2s (former 116 OVTAE), used for parachute training of airborne troops, and based at Ulyanovsk, was also assigned to the new regiment. Colonel Vadim Dyrdin, previously commanding the 116 OVTAE, was appointed chief of the 235 VTAP. Later, the new Il-76MD-90 aircraft produced by Aviastar-SP, and the An-124 aircraft undergoing overhauls at the same facility, will be assigned to the 235 VTAP. On 2 April 2019, the regiment received its

Three new Il-22PP Porubshchik jamming aircraft are on strength with the 117th Military Transport Aviation Regiment at Orenburg. This is Il-22PP RF-90786. (Piotr Butowski)

first Il-76MD-90A (RF-78655), the first aircraft of this type delivered to an operational unit. The airfield of Ulyanovsk Vostochnyi has a vast runway, 5,150m (16,896ft) long and 110m (361ft) wide.

The 235 VTAP existed once previously, during 1989–98, when it operated An-124 and Il-76 aircraft. Since there were no funds to sustain the airworthiness of the An-124s, the regiment was disbanded in 1998. The regimental day of the first 235 VTAP was 1 October; it is likely the re-established unit will retain this date.

708th Military Transport Aviation Regiment (708 VTAP)
Location: Taganrog
Commanding officer: Colonel Ivan Zolot'ko

This unit was formed on 7 October 1942; since 1987 it has operated Il-76MD aircraft. During 1960–92 the regiment was based in Gantsa, Azerbaijan; after its return to Russia the regiment was deployed to Taganrog. Currently the regiment operates around 20 Il-76MDs. The airfield at Taganrog Tsentralnyi has a runway 2,500m (8,202ft) long and 45m (148ft) wide (there is another airfield in Taganrog, occupied by the Beriev company).

The 708 VTAP received the titles Guard and Kerch in 1995, when it received the traditions of the disbanded 192 VTAP (based at Ukurey near Baikal). The regimental day is 7 October.

As the only airborne early warning unit in Russia, the Aviation Squadron of Long-Range Radar Surveillance Aircraft is responsible for A-50U RF-50610 '42 Red', delivered on 28 March 2019.
(Beriev)

610th Combat Application and Flight Crew Conversion Centre (610 TsBP PLS)

Location: Ivanovo Severnyi
Commanding officer: Colonel Vladimir Rybkin

This centre has its origins in the 25th VTA Officer Course, established on 1 September 1967; it has been based at Ivanovo since 1968. On 1 January 1974 the centre received its current name. The centre bears the name of Marshal Nikolai Skripko, a former long-time commander of the VTA. The centre's day is marked on 1 September.

The centre is tasked with increasing the qualifications of transport aircraft and ground crews, and transport aircraft commanders, as well as conducting research into transport aviation applications. The centre has a squadron of Il-76 aircraft, as well as single transport aircraft of other types: An-22, An-26, An-72 and Il-18. A squadron of An-2s for parachute training of airborne troops is based at the same airfield. The airfield of Ivanovo Severnyi (North) has a runway 2,300m (7,546ft) long and 40m (131ft) wide.

A part of the centre is the **Aviation Squadron of Long-Range Radar Surveillance Aircraft** commanded by Lieutenant Colonel Valentin Kovalyov, the only airborne early warning and control (AEW&C) unit in Russia. It was formed on 20 May 1966 with Tu-126 aircraft; in November 1988, along with the arrival of the A-50 aircraft, the squadron was expanded to regiment size and in 1998 it was re-formed into the 2457th Aviation Base. In 2009 the base lost its independence and was assigned to the 610th Centre at Ivanovo. It is probable that the squadron will be expanded to a regiment after the launch of production of the new A-100 AEW&C aircraft, which may be expected after 2023. For the time being the squadron has only 10 airworthy A-50s (including six upgraded A-50U versions, the latest example delivered in March 2019). Nine more A-50s have been standing on the periphery of Ivanovo airfield and have not been flown for many years.

An-2 aircraft squadrons

On 1 January 2010 the Russian Air Force took over seven independent military transport aviation squadrons (OVTAE) previously assigned to the Airborne Troops; since then the VDV has had no organic air units. In 2013, the Krymsk-based 185 OVTAE was disbanded. Two other squadrons have been subordinated to 'large' VTA regiments: the former 340 OVTAE in Omsk now belongs to the 117 VTAP in Orenburg and the former 116 OVTAE in Ulyanovsk became part of the newly formed 235 VTAP. The remaining four squadrons are probably still independent and subordinated directly to VTA command. These squadrons are located at the stations of airborne divisions, brigades and training centres and are used for parachute training. Each squadron has around 10 An-2 aircraft; an additional pair of An-26 medium transport aircraft and a flight of Mi-8 helicopters is based at Ryazan.

A detailed ORBAT table of all Military Transport Aviation units can be found on page 52.

223rd and 224th Flight Detachments

Under orders from the president of Russia dated 15 January 1993, two commercial structures, the 223rd and 224th Flight Detachments (Lyotnyi Otryad, LO) were established and registered as aviation companies. They provide air transport services for Russian government customers, presidential administration, the Rosoboronexport arms trade company, etc.

The 223 LO was detached from the 8 ADON in Chkalovsky; it operates more than 20 Il-62, Il-76, Tu-134 and Tu-154 aircraft.

The 224 LO took over aircraft from the 12 VTAD; the company is based in Tver. According to an official register, in January 2018 the 224 LO operated two An-124-100 and 11 Il-76MD aircraft.

The 224th Flight Detachment operates 11 Il-76MD aircraft from its base at Tver, including RA-78844. The unit also has a pair of An-124-100s. (Piotr Butowski)

Aviation units assigned as direct reporting units, to Long-range Aviation and to Military Transport Aviation

Direct reporting units

Formation	HQ	Inventory
8 ADON	Chkalovsky	Transports, special duty aircraft
SAP (ON)	Hmeimim, Syria	Tactical aircraft, helicopters, reconnaissance component

Evaluation and crew conversion centres

Formation	Unit	HQ/Location	Inventory
929 GLITs MO RF		Akhtubinsk	Combat aircraft under state evaluation; a squadron of MiG-31K Kinzhal strike aircraft
4 GTs PAP VI MO RF		Lipetsk	
	968 IISAP	Lipetsk	MiG-29 (1 sqn), Su-24/Su-34 (1 sqn), Su-25 (1 sqn), Su-27/Su-30SM/Su-35S (1 sqn), An-26 (1 det)
	AE	Savasleyka	MiG-31 (1 sqn)
	237 TsPAT	Kubinka	MiG-29 (1 sqn), Su-30SM (1sqn), An-30 (1 det), Il-20
344 GTsBP PLS AA		Torzhok	
	696 IIVP	Torzhok	Helicopters
	92 (?) IIVE	Klin	Mi-8/Mi-24 (1 sqn)
924 GTs BpA MO RF		Kolomna	Unmanned vehicles
185 TsBP BPr VKS		Astrakhan	
	116 UTsBPr IA	Privolzhsky (Astrakhan)	MiG-29 (2 sqn), Mi-8/An-26 (1 sqn)

Training aviation bases of the Krasnodar Military Aviation College of Pilots

Base	Location	Inventory
192 UAvB	Tikhoretsk	L-39C
195 UAvB	Kushchovskaya	L-39C, Yak-130, MiG-29, Su-25, Su-27
200 UAvB	Armavir	L-39C, Yak-130, MiG-29
205 UAvB	Balashov	An-26
209 UAvB	Borisoglebsk	Yak-130, Su-25
213 UAvB	Kotelnikovo	L-39C
217 UAvB	Rtishchevo	L-410
219 UAvB	Michurinsk	L-39C
272 UAvB	Maykop	L-39C

Long-Range Aviation Command

Formation	Unit	HQ/Location	Inventory
22 TBAD		Engels	
	121 TBAP	Engels	Tu-95MS (1 sqn), Tu-160 (1 sqn)
	52 TBAP	Shaykovka	Tu-22M3 (2 sqn)
	40 SAP	Vysokiy (Olenyegorsk)	Tu-22M3 (1 sqn), transports
326 TBAD		Ukrainka (Seryshevo)	
	182 TBAP	Ukrainka (Seryshevo)	Tu-95MS (3 sqn)
	200 TBAP	Belaya near Irkutsk	Tu-22M3 (2 sqn), An-30 (1 det)
43 TsBP PLS DA		Dyagilevo (Ryazan)	An-26, Tu-22M3, Tu-95MS, Tu-134UBL
	27 SAP	Tambov	An-26 (1sqn), Tu-134UBL (1 sqn)
203 OAP SZ		Dyagilevo (Ryazan)	Il-78/Il-78M (2 sqn)

Military Transport Aviation

Formation	Unit	HQ/Location	Inventory
12 VTAD		Migalovo (Tver)	
	196 VTAP	Migalovo (Tver)	Il-76 (2 sqn), An-22 (1 det)
	334 VTAP	Kresty (Pskov)	Il-76 (2 sqn)
	566 VTAP	Seshcha (Bryansk)	An-124 (1 sqn), Il-76 (1 sqn)
18 VTAD		Orenburg	
	117 VTAP	Orenburg	An-12PPS/Il-22PP (1 sqn), Il-76 (2 sqn)
		Omsk	An-2 (1 sqn), An-26, An-72
	235 VTAP	Ulyanovsk Vostochnyi	An-2 (1 sqn), Il-76 (1 sqn), An-124 (1 det)
	708 VTAP	Taganrog	Il-76 (2 sqn)
610 TsBP PLS		Ivanovo Severnyi	A-50 (1 sqn), An-2 (1 sqn), Il-76 (1 sqn), other transports

An-2 aircraft independent squadrons	Unit	Location
Ryazan Institute of Airborne Troops, Ryazan	58 OVTAE	Dyagilevo (Ryazan)
76th Airborne-Assault Division, Pskov	242 OVTAE	Kresty (Pskov)
98th Airborne Division, Ivanovo	243 OVTAE	Ivanovo Severnyi
106th Airborne Division, Tula	110 OVTAE	Klokovo (Tula)

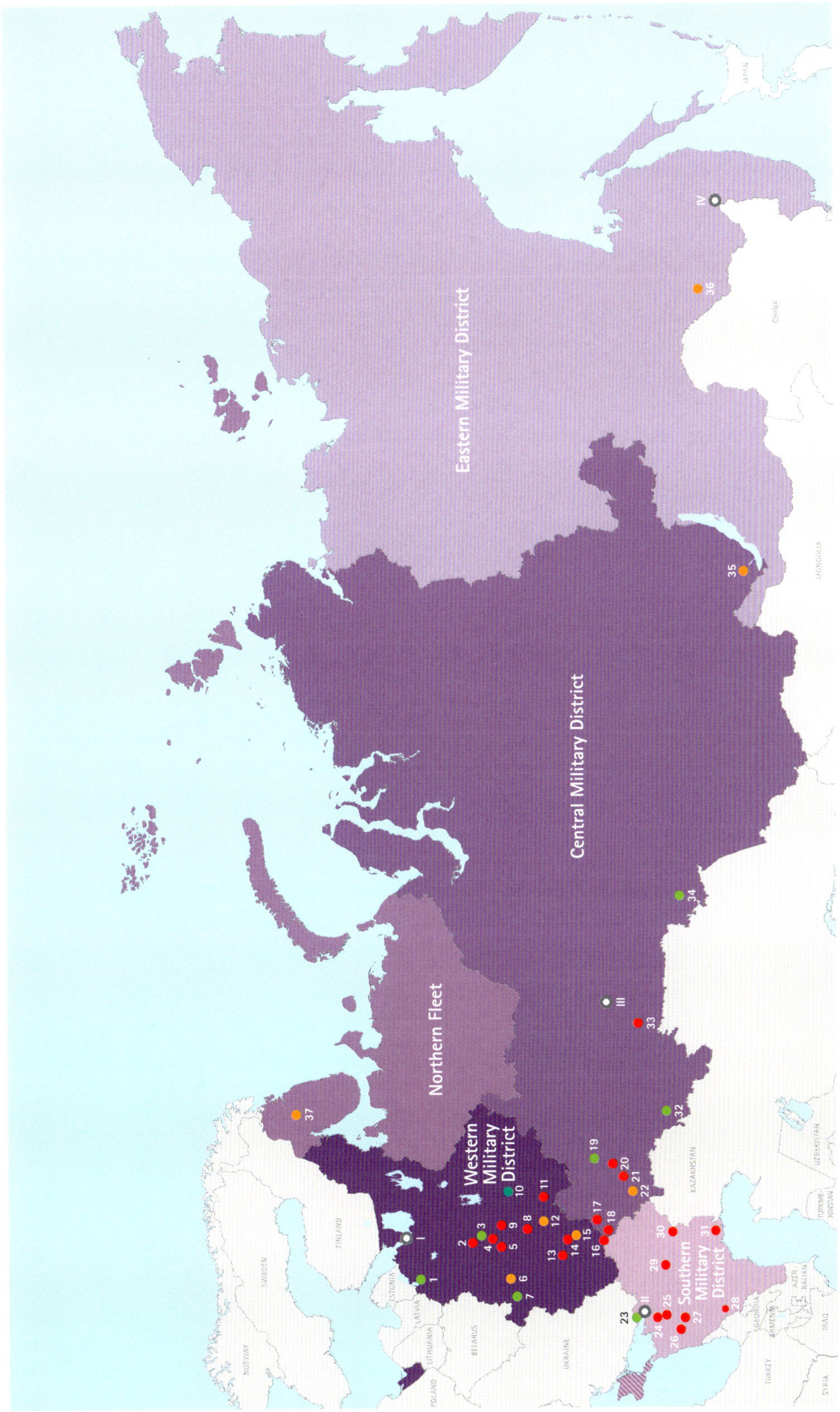

Military District HQ

I	St Petersburg (Western MD)
II	Rostov-on-Don (Southern MD)
III	Yekaterinburg (Central MD)
IV	Khabarovsk (Eastern MD)

VVS Bases

1	Kresty (Pskov)
2	Torzhok
3	Migalovo (Tver)
4	Klin
5	Kubinka
6	Shaykovka
7	Seshcha (Bryansk)
8	Kolomna
9	Chkalovsky
10	Ivanovo Severnyi
11	Savasleyka
12	Dyagilevo (Ryazan)
13	Lipetsk
14	Michurinsk
15	Tambov
16	Borisoglebsk
17	Rtishchevo
18	Balashov
19	Ulyanovsk Vostochnyi
20	Syzran
21	Volsk
22	Engels
23	Taganrog
24	Kushchovskaya
25	Tikhoretsk
26	Maykop
27	Armavir
28	Nalchik
29	Kotelnikovo
30	Akhtubinsk
31	Astrakhan
32	Orenburg
33	Chelyabinsk
34	Omsk
35	Belaya
36	Ukrainka (Seryshevo)
37	Vysokiy (Olenyegorsk)

Key

- Military District HQ
- Direct Reporting Bases
- Long-Range Aviation Command (DA)
- Military Transport Aviation (VTA)
- occupied territory

A map of direct reporting units, Long-range Aviation and Military Transport Aviation. (Map by James Lawrence)

4th Air Force and Air Defence Army (4 A VVS PVO)

HQ: Rostov-on-Don
Commanding officer: Major General Nikolay Gostev

The 4th Air Army of the Soviet Air Force was formed on 22 May 1942. After World War II it remained in Polish territory. In 1992 the HQ was moved to Rostov-on-Don and the army complement was formed of units withdrawn from Belarus, Germany and Poland. In 2009 the 4th Army was transformed into 4th AF and AD Command (absorbing some units of the disbanded 5th AF and AD Army in Yekaterinburg) and on 1 August 2015 it was transformed again into the 4th AF and AD Army. This army is subordinated to the Joint Strategic Command of the Southern Military District and has been awarded the Red Banner order.

Units of the 4th Army bore the brunt of the fighting in Chechnya in the 1990s and early 2000s, later taking part in the war with Georgia in 2008 and seizure of Crimea in 2014. Currently they are kept in readiness in case of escalation of the conflict with Ukraine. The 4th Army includes a powerful air strike component: two regiments of Su-24/Su-34 tactical bombers, two regiments of Su-25 attack aircraft, plus a brigade and two regiments of army helicopters. On the other hand, it does not include any MiG-31 interceptor units, which are of little to no value for operations in the south of Russia. Additionally, in 2014 a new composite division, the 27 SAD, with three aviation regiments, was established within the 4th Army in captured Crimea.

Apart from air units, the 4th Army includes the 51st Air Defence Division with three regiments of SAMs in Rostov-on-Don (S-300PM), Sochi (Buk) and Novorossiysk (S-400, Pantsir-S) as well as the 31st AD Division in Crimea with two missile regiments in Sevastopol (S-400) and Feodosia (S-400, S-300PM, Pantsir-S).

Two foreign bases are subordinated to the Southern MD: the 102nd Military Base in Armenia (its air component is the 3624 AvB described below) and the 7th Military Base in Abkhazia (Georgia). The latter has no permanent air component but maintains a duty post at Gudauta airfield. Sub-units of four to six helicopters, usually Mi-8s, but also Ka-52s or Mi-26s, are periodically deployed there. The link between the 4th Army's HQ and subordinated troops is the **214th Management Centre** (Tsentr Upravleniya) in Novocherkassk, 30km (19 miles) northeast of Rostov.

1st Composite Aviation Division (1 SAD)

HQ: Krymsk
Commanding officer: Major General Sergey Rumyantsev

The 1 SAD was formed on 11 November 2013 by re-forming the 6972 AvB (1st Grade) in Krymsk; air groups from the base were transformed into regiments. The 1 SAD had did existed during 1943–2009, but the new division in Krymsk is only loosely related to it. The traditions – the Guard and Baranovichi (a town in Belarus) titles and the Red Banner and Suvorov 2nd Grade orders – were inherited by the new 1 SAD division from the renowned 209th Fighter Aviation Regiment, disbanded in 2001 in Astrakhan (see 3 SAP). The divisional holiday is 21 October, marking the date of the 209 IAP's formation in 1941.

3rd Composite Aviation Regiment (3 SAP)
Location: Krymsk
Commanding officer: Lieutenant Colonel Oleg Zakharov

The current 3 SAP was formed on 1 September 2001 at Krymsk air base through the merger of two disbanded units, the 562 IAP based at Krymsk and the 209 IAP based at Astrakhan; both had operated Su-27s. The new unit was named 3 IAP in honour of a renowned regiment with the same number, disbanded in 1992. On 24 August 2009, the 3 IAP and 178th Detachment of Ka-27 rescue helicopters, also based at Krymsk, were merged into the 6972 AvB, which was transformed into the 3 SAP on 1 December 2013. Currently the regiment maintains no formal traditions, although the previous 3 SAP had carried the Guard and Rostov-Don titles until 2009.

During 2010–11 the unit received a squadron of 12 new-production Su-27SM(3) fighters and then, during 2014–18, another squadron of aircraft upgraded to Su-27SM(3) standard. As of the end of 2018 the regiment had two squadrons of Su-27SM(3) fighters and a handful of Su-30M2 trainers, one squadron of non-upgraded Su-27s, as well as a detachment of Ka-27s. During 2012–14 the runway at Krymsk underwent reconstruction (during that period the regiment was deployed to Millerovo); currently the runway is 3,000m (9,843ft) long and 62m (203ft) wide.

31st Fighter Aviation Regiment (31 IAP)
Location: Millerovo
Commanding officer: Lieutenant Colonel Aleksey Khasanov

Until 2009, the MiG-29-equipped 19 IAP was based at Millerovo. In 2009 it was transformed into the 6969 AvB and in 2010 into an air group of the 6972 AvB. At that time the MiG-29s from the disbanded 31 IAP based at Zernograd, 240km (149 miles) south of Millerovo, were transferred to the base. In December 2014 the aviation group at

Millerovo is home to the 31st Fighter Aviation Regiment and Su-30SM RF-95819 '03 Red', seen trailing its twin brake parachutes. (Piotr Butowski)

Milerovo was transformed once again, into a fighter regiment. It was given the number 31, but assumed the traditions of the 19 IAP, including the regimental holiday on 19 January. Amid the turmoil of transformations, the regiment has lost these traditions, although both the 19 IAP and 31 IAP had been regiments of the Guard in the past. Between October 2015 and November 2018 the regiment received two full squadrons of Su-30SMs (24 aircraft), which replaced the MiG-29s. There are around 25 MiG-29s still standing at the base, but they are no longer in active service.

559th Bomber Aviation Regiment (559 BAP)

Location: Morozovsk
Commanding officer: Colonel Anatoly Stolbinsky

This unit was formed on 15 July 1950; until 1993 it was based in Germany and then it was withdrawn to Morozovsk. In 1993 the regiment received Su-24M aircraft from the disbanded 143 BAP, withdrawn from Georgia at that time. In September 2009 the Morozovsk-based 559 BAP was merged with the reconnaissance 11 ORAP based at Marinovka to create the 6970th Aviation Base. At that time, Su-24Ms from the disbanded regiments 722 BAP (Smuravyevo) and 959 BAP (Yeysk) were transferred to Morozovsk. In December 2011 the 6970 AvB became an aviation group and part of the 6972 AvB. Eventually, in December 2013, the unit became a regiment again, for some time the independent 559 OBAP and then the 559 BAP.

Between October 2013 and November 2015 the Morozovsk regiment was re-equipped with Su-34 aircraft; currently it has three squadrons with a total of 36 Su-34s. More than 20 unserviceable Su-24Ms are still present at the base. During a visit to the unit in July 2017, Lieutenant General Andrey Yudin announced that the Morozovsk regiment would be the first to receive upgraded Su-34M aircraft. The Su-34s of the 559 BAP have seen service in Syria. The regimental holiday is 15 July. The runway at Morozovsk is 2,550m (8,366ft) long and 40m (131ft) wide.

4th Composite Aviation Division (4 SAD)

HQ: Marinovka (Volgograd)

This is a new division, the HQ of which was established in around 2016.

11th Composite Aviation Regiment (11 SAP)

Location: Marinovka (Volgograd)

The 11th Reconnaissance Regiment was formed on 1 August 1942 (marked today as the regimental holiday). In 2009, the 11 ORAP was merged with the 559 BAP, creating a single aviation base. In December 2013 the unit based at Marinovka regained independence as the 2nd Independent Reconnaissance Aviation Squadron. During 2014–15 the Su-24M bombers from Morozovsk were transferred to Marinovka (Morozovsk meanwhile received new Su-34s). In this way, on 1 December 2015 the squadron was expanded to regiment size and named the 11 OSAP and then, after having become a

Su-25UB RF-92256 '97 Red' is a two-seat combat trainer from the 368th Attack Aviation Regiment based at Budyonnovsk. (Piotr Butowski)

part of the division, the SAP. The runway at Marinovka is 2,500m (8,202ft) long and 50m (164ft) wide. In 2017 the runway surface was renewed and the taxiways widened.

368th Attack Aviation Regiment (368 ShAP)
Location: Budyonnovsk
Commanding officer: Lieutenant Colonel Yuri Petrov

This regiment was created on 12 July 1984 in Ukraine, with the then new Su-25 attack aircraft. During 1986–87 one squadron from the regiment operated in Afghanistan. Between 1988 and 1993 the regiment was based in East Germany and then took part in the fighting in Chechnya. At the same, Budyonnovsk was home to a helicopter regiment, the 487 OVP. During the turbulent period of 2009–11 both units were merged into the 6971 AvB and then split again. In 2014 the 368 ShAP transferred one of its Su-25SM squadrons to the newly created 37 SAP based at Gvardeyskoye in Crimea; it currently has two squadrons equipped with Su-25SM and Su-25SM3 aircraft.

960th Attack Aviation Regiment (960 ShAP)
Location: Primorsko-Akhtarsk

This unit was formed on 25 March 1955 at Primorsko-Akhtarsk as the 960th Training Aviation Regiment. In February 1993 it was transformed into the 960 IAP and received

MiG-29 fighters from units withdrawn from Lithuania (53 IAP) and Georgia (176 IAP). On 1 May 1998 the regiment was re-equipped again, this time with Su-25 attack aircraft from the disbanded 16 ShAP based at Taganrog, and was renamed the 960 ShAP. From 1999 the 960 ShAP fought in Chechnya and saw combat in Georgia in 2008. On 1 December 2009 the regiment was transformed into the 6973 AvB; at the same time a group of Su-25s from the disbanded 461 ShAP based at Krasnodar was redeployed to Primorsko-Akhtarsk. A year later the base was transformed into an aviation group within the 6972 AvB, with its HQ in Krymsk. On 10 January 2014 the group was transformed once again into a regiment and the name 960 ShAP was restored.

27th Composite Aviation Division (27 SAD)

HQ: Belbek (Sevastopol, Crimea, Ukraine)

Immediately after the seizure of Crimea by Russia in 2014, the headquarters of a new air force division, the 27 SAD, was formed. This had three newly formed regiments – the 37th Composite, 38th Fighter and 39th Helicopter – subordinated to it.

37th Composite Aviation Regiment (37 SAP)

Location: Gvardeyskoye
Commanding officer: Colonel Oleg Terebunsky

This is a new regiment formed at Gvardeyskoye, formerly the home of the 43 OMShAP of the Russian Black Sea Fleet, a regiment that has since redeployed to Saki, also in Crimea. The 37th Regiment has two squadrons – a bomber unit with Su-24M aircraft taken from the Morozovsk-based 559 BAP, and an attack unit with Su-25SM aircraft

The 960th Attack Aviation Regiment at Primorsko-Akhtarsk includes upgraded Su-25SM3 aircraft – this is RF-95482 '92 Red'. (Piotr Butowski)

Among the more recent additions to the 4th Army is the 39th Helicopter Regiment at Dzhankoy. Its inventory includes Mi-28N RF-95576 '41 Blue'. (Piotr Butowski)

inherited from the Primorsko-Akhtarsk-based 960 ShAP; Oleg Terebunsky, the previous 960 ShAP chief, was appointed commander of the 37 SAP. Gvardeyskoye air base has a runway 3,100m (10,171ft) long and 80m (262ft) wide.

38th Fighter Aviation Regiment (38 IAP)
Location: Belbek

The 38 IAP was formed in 2014. It has two squadrons of Su-27 and Su-27UB fighters transferred from several units, mostly from the 3 SAP based at Krymsk.
The runway at Belbek air base is 3,050m (10,007ft) long and 60m (197ft) wide.

The 38th Fighter Aviation Regiment was established at the former Ukrainian Air Force base of Belbek in Crimea. Su-27 RF-95943 '09 Blue' is one of the unit's fighters. (Piotr Butowski)

The 30th Independent Transport Composite Aviation Regiment at Rostov-on-Don operates a mixed fleet of fixed-wing transports and helicopters, including An-12 RF-95685 '25 Blue'. (Piotr Butowski)

39th Helicopter Regiment (39 VP)
Location: Dzhankoy
Commanding officer: Colonel Oleg Panin

This regiment was formed on 3 July 2014. The first squadron, with Ka-52 helicopters, arrived from the 55 OVP based at Korenovsk. Later, the second squadron, equipped with Mi-28Ns and Mi-35Ms, and a third squadron with the Mi-8AMTSh were formed; the squadrons are not currently complete. The runway at Dzhankoy is 2,500m (8,202ft) long and 55m (180ft) wide.

30th Independent Transport Composite Aviation Regiment (30 OTSAP)

Location: Rostov-on-Don

This is a transport aviation unit serving the HQs of the Southern MD and the 4th Army; it comprises a fixed-wing aircraft squadron with a dozen An-12 and An-26 aircraft, single An-148, Il-22, L-410 and Tu-134 aircraft, as well as a helicopter squadron with a dozen Mi-8 and Mi-26 helicopters. The duty post at Adler (Sochi) airfield is subordinated to the regiment. The runway at Rostov is 2,500m (8,202ft) long and 45m (148ft) wide.

3624th Aviation Base (3624 AvB)

Location: Erebuni, Armenia
Commanding officer: Colonel Alexander Petrov

Russia maintains the 102nd Military Base in the town of Gyumri in Armenian territory (during the Soviet era this was was home to the 127th Infantry Division of the Soviet Army). The base is subordinated to the Southern MD; in accordance with an agreement of 2010 Russia is entitled to retain forces here until 2044. The air component at Erebuni was formed on 12 July 1995 as the 426th Aviation Group, with six MiG-23 fighters, replaced from 1998 by MiG-29s. In July 2001 the group was expanded to become the 3624th Aviation Base; it has one squadron of 18 MiG-29 fighters and one of Mi-8 and Mi-24 helicopters. In April 2019 it was announced that the MiG-29s at Erebuni will be replaced by 18 Su-30SM fighters by 2020–21.

3661st Aviation Base (3661 AvB)

Location: Mozdok

Mozdok air base in North Ossetia is particularly important for Russia, in order to control the situation in the Caucasus. It is located near Ingushetia and Chechnya, two regions of Russia that remain unstable; Grozny, the capital of Chechnya, is 100km (62 miles) away. Mozdok air base was extensively used by the Russian Air Force in both Chechen wars and the conflict with Georgia in 2008 (the Georgian border is slightly more than 100km away). As the southernmost large Russian air base, since 2015 Mozdok has been used for refuelling stops by aircraft bound for Hmeimim base in Syria. The Tu-22M3 bombers attacking Syria also operate from Mozdok.

In response to the Syrian campaign, a significant enlargement of the base began in 2015. A new runway (3,500 × 60m; 11,483 × 197ft) was built in parallel to the old runway (3,500 × 70m; 11,483 × 230ft). As of autumn 2018, the new runway was complete; most taxiways, aircraft hardstands, communication roads, buildings and other infrastructure were still to be built. Until 1998 Mozdok was a base for Tu-95MS strategic bombers. Currently only Mi-8s and Mi-24s of the FSB and Federal National Guard Service are permanently based here, as well as a squadron of Forpost UAVs belonging to the 487 OVP.

16th Army Aviation Brigade (16 Br AA)

Location: Zernograd

On 1 December 2015 the new 16th Army Aviation Brigade was formed at Zernograd air base (which had been non-operational since 2009). The core of the new brigade was provided by the 546 AvB AA in Rostov-on-Don, formed in 2010 using personnel and

MiG-29 RF-92262 '01 Red' is one of the few first-generation 'Fulcrums' remaining in VKS service and is based at Erebuni's 3624th Aviation Base. (Russian MoD)

equipment from several disbanded units in the vicinity of that town, mainly the 325th Helicopter Regiment in Yegorlykskaya.

In summer 2012, when it was still the 546 AvB AA in Rostov, the unit received its first Mi-28N and then Mi-35M attack helicopters (both types are produced by the Rostvertol plant in Rostov). The brigade has two squadrons of Mi-8 transport helicopters (including the new Mi-8AMTSh), two squadrons of Mi-28N and Mi-35M attack helicopters and a detachment of Mi-26 heavy helicopters. Around a dozen old Mi-8s and a few non-airworthy Mi-26 helicopters (without rotor blades) remain on the airfield. The runway at Zernograd, unchanged for many years, is 2,500m (8,202ft) long and 40m (131ft) wide; before the brigade was deployed there, only the buildings had been refurbished.

55th Independent Helicopter Regiment (55 OVP)

Location: Korenovsk
Commanding officer: Colonel Yevgeny Sukhodolsky

This unit's history dates back to 1942; it has been based at Korenovsk since 1992. In January 2010 the regiment was transformed into the 6974 AvB, in November 2010 it became the 393 AvB AA, and on 1 December 2015 it was again transformed into the 55 OVP regiment. The regiment's crews have taken part in all the conflicts that the USSR

A Mi-8AMTSh of the 16th Army Aviation Brigade, photographed in 2018. The brigade includes two squadrons flying the 'Hip'. (Russian MoD)

Mi-28N RF-91344 '12 Red', of the 55th Independent Helicopter Regiment based at Korenovsk, seen in December 2018. (Russian MoD)

and Russia have been involved in, including Afghanistan, Chechnya, Dagestan, Georgia and Syria. According to the official history 'the regiment actively participated in the returning of Crimea into the Russian Federation'. On 8 July 2016, Colonel Ryafagat Khabibullin, the then commander of the 55 OVP, was killed in Syria flying a Mi-35M. The regiment has the title Sevastopol and Kutuzov order; the regimental day is 20 March.

The 55 OVP currently has a squadron of Mi-8AMTSh transport helicopters (the first examples arrived in 2010), a squadron of Mi-28N (October 2010) and Mi-35M (2012) attack helicopters, and a squadron of Ka-52 attack helicopters. The Ka-52 squadron has actually been formed twice, the first time in 2013. After the seizure of Crimea in 2014 the squadron was moved to Dzhankoy to begin forming the new 39 VP. The Korenovsk regiment obtained a new Ka-52 squadron in 2016. During 2013–16 major reconstruction of the airfield was conducted – in fact, it was rebuilt from scratch. A concrete runway measuring 2,600 × 42m (8,530 × 138ft) was built (previously there was a grass strip, as well as sheltered parking areas for helicopters, which is unique in Russia.

487th Independent Helicopter Regiment (487 OVP)

Location: Budyonnovsk
Commanding officer: Colonel Yuri Borisikov

The 487 OVP was formed in 1989 in East Germany; in August 1993 it was redeployed to Budyonnovsk. In 2009 the regiment was merged with a Su-25 attack aircraft regiment also based there to create the single 6971 AvB, but two years later the fixed-wing aircraft and helicopters were separated. On 1 December 2011 the 387 AvB AA was formed from the helicopters, and on 1 December 2015 the base was transformed back into the 487 OVP regiment.

Currently the regiment has a transport squadron with Mi-8AMTSh and Mi-8MTV-5 helicopters and two combat squadrons with Mi-24, Mi-28N (the first arrived in March 2009) and Mi-35M (since 2012) attack helicopters. The squadron of Forpost UAVs based at Mozdok (120km, 75 miles south of Budyonnovsk) and a duty post at Khankala (Grozny) airfield are subordinated to the regiment.

Aviation units assigned to the Southern Military District/4th Air Force and Air Defence Army

Formation	Unit	HQ/Location	Inventory
1 SAD		Krymsk	
	3 SAP	Krymsk	Su-27SM3/Su-30M2 (2 sqn), Su-27 (1 sqn), Ka-27 (1 det)
	31 IAP	Millerovo	Su-30SM (2 sqn)
	559 BAP	Morozovsk	Su-34 (3 sqn)
4 SAD		Marinovka (Volgograd)	
	11 SAP	Marinovka (Volgograd)	Su-24M (2 sqn), Su-24MR (1 sqn)
	368 ShAP	Budyonnovsk	Su-25SM/SM3 (2 sqn)
	960 ShAP	Primorsko-Akhtarsk	Su-25SM/SM3 (2 sqn)
27 SAD		Belbek (Crimea, Ukraine)	
	37 SAP	Gvardeyskoye	Su-24M (1 sqn), Su-25SM (1 sqn)
	38 IAP	Belbek	Su-27 (2 sqn)
	39 VP	Dzhankoy	Ka-52 (1 sqn), Mi-8AMTSh (1 sqn), Mi-28N/Mi-35M (1 sqn)
30 OTSAP		Rostov-on-Don	Special transports
3624 AvB		Erebuni, Armenia	MiG-29 (1 sqn), Mi-8/Mi-24 (1 sqn)
3661AvB		Mozdok	
16 Br AA		Zernograd	Mi-8/Mi-8AMTSh (2 sqn), Mi-28N/Mi-35M (2 sqn), Mi-26 (1 det)
55 OVP		Korenovsk	Ka-52 (1 sqn), Mi-8AMTSh (1 sqn), Mi-28N/Mi-35M (1 sqn)
487 OVP		Budyonnovsk	Mi-8AMTSh/MTV-5 (1 sqn), Mi-24/Mi-28N/Mi-35M (2 sqn)
		Mozdok	Forpost UAV (1 sqn)

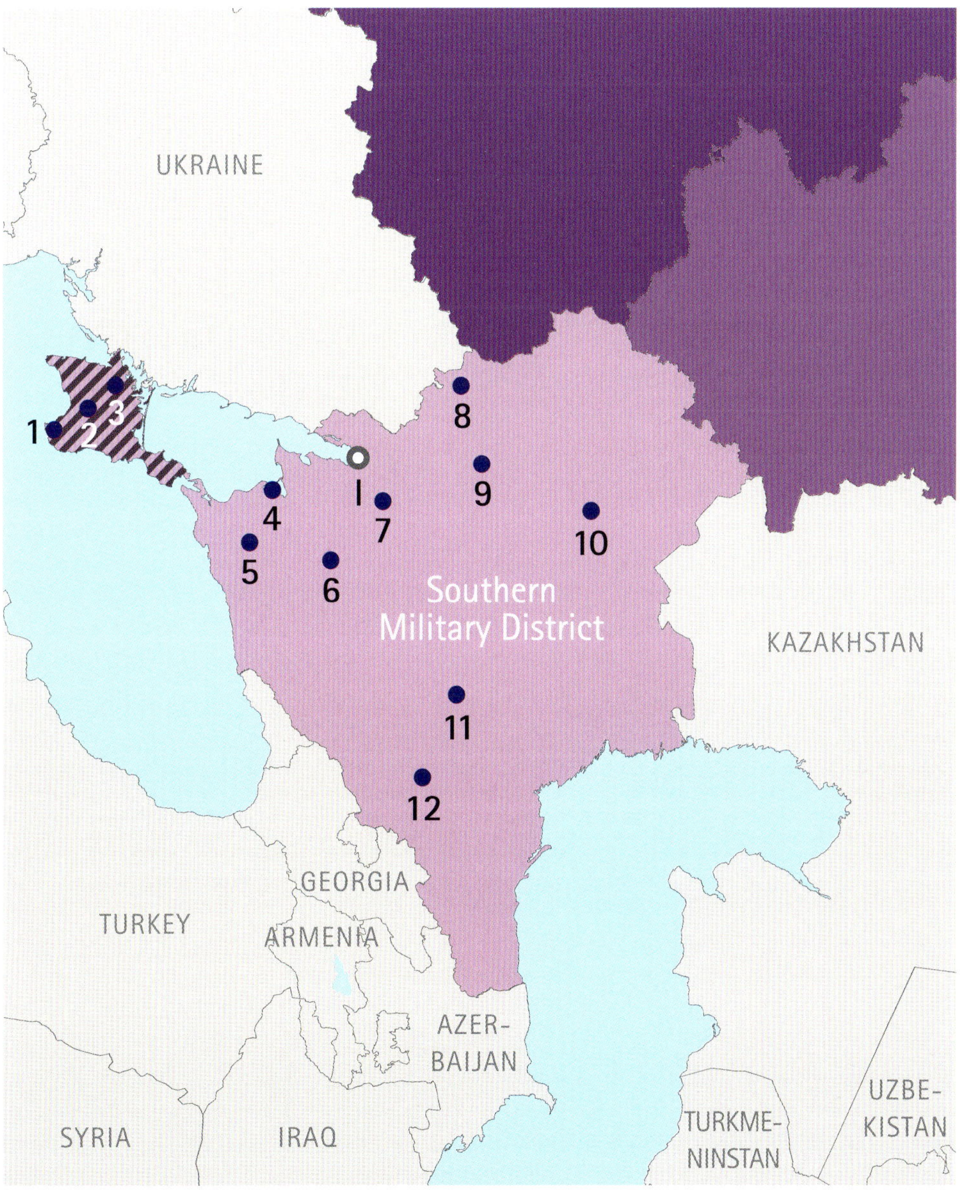

Military District HQ

I Rostov-on-Don

VVS Bases

1 Belbek (Ukraine)
2 Gvardeyskoye
3 Dzhankoy
4 Primorsko-Akhtarsk
5 Krymsk
6 Korenovsk
7 Zernograd
8 Millerovo
9 Morozovsk
10 Marinovka (Volgograd)
11 Budyonnovsk
12 Mozdok

Key

Military District HQ
VVS Base

occupied territory

A map of the Southern Military District and the 4th Air Force and Air Defence Army. (Map by James Lawrence)

6th Air Force and Air Defence Army (6 A VVS PVO)

HQ: St Petersburg
Commanding officer: Lieutenant General Alexander Duplinsky

This army was formed by the merger of three previous armies: the 6th, 16th and 76th; the unit number and most of the traditions were inherited from the 6th Independent Air Defence Army with its HQ in St Petersburg (Leningrad), formed on 5 April 1942. During 2009–15 it was the 1st AF and AD Command with its HQ in Voronezh. In 2015, along with the transformation into an army, the HQ was moved to St Petersburg. The 6 A VVS PVO is subordinated to the Joint Strategic Command of the Western MD. The 6th Army has the title Leningrad and Red Banner order.

In the past this army had a very potent air defence component: both interceptors and SAM regiments. It had two tasks: protection of the most industrialised, European part of the USSR against attacks from the north (this task was conducted by MiG-31s), as well as protection of nuclear-powered submarines, departing their base on the Kola peninsula (conducted by Su-27s). Now little of this remains.

Apart from the air units, the 6th Army includes the 2nd AD Division with its HQ in St Petersburg and five SAM regiments based in Zelenogorsk (S-400, S-300PS), Gostilitsy (S-400, Pantsir-S), Vaganovo (S-400, Pantsir-S), Vaskelovo (Buk, S-300V) and Ulyanovka (S-300PS), plus the 32nd AD Division with its HQ in Tver and two missile regiments in Izhintsy (S-300PS) and Voronezh (S-300PM).

The link between the 6th Army's HQ and subordinated troops is the 213th Management Centre (Tsentr Upravleniya) in Khvoyny (St Petersburg).

105th Composite Aviation Division (105 SAD)

HQ: Voronezh
Commanding officer: Colonel Sergey Prokofyev

The division was formed in 1950; during 1960–93 it was based in East Germany. On 10 August 1993 the division's HQ was moved to Voronezh. In 2009 the division was transformed into the 7000th Aviation Base and on 1 December 2013 it became the 105 SAD again. The division has the Guard, Borisov and Pomerania titles, as well as the Red Banner (awarded twice) and Suvorov orders, inherited in 2009 from the disbanded 47 ORAP.

14th Fighter Aviation Regiment (14 IAP)

Location: Khalino (Kursk)
Commanding officer: Lieutenant Colonel Maxim Sevostyanov

This regiment was formed on 7 March 1938. During 1957-91 it was based in Hungary. In 1991 it was withdrawn to Zherdyevka and in 1999 it was moved to Khalino air base near Kursk. In 2009 the regiment obtained 28 MiG-29SMT fighters that had been refused by Algeria. In 2009 the regiment was transformed into the 6963 AvB, in 2010 into the 5 AvGr 7000 AvB, and in 2013 into the 14 IAP once again. The regiment has Guard and

Leningrad titles as well as the Red Banner and Suvorov 3rd Grade orders. During the (fairly provisional) renovation of Khalino air base in 2010–12 the regiment was based at Buturlinovka. The runway at Khalino is 2,500m (8,202ft) long and 40m (131ft) wide.

Between June 2017 and December 2018 the regiment received two 12-aircraft squadrons of Su-30SM fighters. For the time being, some 30 MiG-29s, including SMT versions, remain at the airfield. It is probable the MiG-29SMTs will be transferred to the Privolzhsky conversion centre, which already operates this variant.

47th Composite Aviation Regiment (47 SAP)

Location: Buturlinovka (planned Voronezh)
Commanding officer: Colonel Maxim Yurchenkov

The 47 SAP was formed on 1 May 1953 as the 455th Research Instructor Regiment; since 1954 it has been based in Voronezh at the airfield known as Baltimore. In 2009 the regiment was transformed into the 7000 AvB, with the addition of reconnaissance aircraft – a squadron of Su-24MR and a detachment of MiG-25RB aircraft from the disbanded 47 ORAP based at Shatalovo, as well as a detachment of An-30 photographic reconnaissance aircraft (former 183 ODRAO). In 2010, after the upgrade of the status of the 7000 AvB to 1st Grade, the unit in Voronezh became an aviation group. In 2013 the group was transformed into a composite aviation regiment, receiving the number 47.

Between December 2010 and October 2013, the 47 SAP received two 12-aircraft squadrons of Su-34s, which replaced the Su-24Ms; it was the first operational unit equipped with Su-34s. Following this, the regiment transferred the Su-24MR and An-30

Su-34 RF-95803 '03 Red' from the 47th Composite Aviation Regiment at Buturlinovka is expected to move to Voronezh in future.
(Piotr Butowski)

aircraft to Shatalovo (see below) and the MiG-25s were scrapped. It is unclear why the regiment is still classed as composite despite operating only Su-34s. One theory suggests some of the Su-34s (perhaps one squadron) are intended for other tasks, such as reconnaissance or electronic warfare and have dedicated equipment and a crew training programme.

In 2013 a thorough reconstruction of Voronezh air base began. The work was to be completed by 2015, but by then only the runway had been partially renovated; further work ceased.

In December 2017 the minister of defence Sergey Shoygu announced that rebuilding Voronezh airfield was a priority for 2018, but nothing more happened that year. Along with the start of the reconstruction in November–December 2013, the aircraft and personnel of the 47 SAP were temporarily redeployed to Buturlinovka, 135km (84 miles) southeast of Voronezh; this provisional state continues to this day. The reconstructed runway at Voronezh is 3,600m (11,811ft) long and 62m (203ft) wide; before reconstruction it measured 2,500 × 48m (8,202 × 157ft).

Planned restoration of the 899th Regiment at Buturlinovka

In November 2009 the 47 SAP was redeployed to Buturlinovka for the duration of the Voronezh reconstruction. Until then, the 899th Attack Aviation Regiment with Su-25 aircraft was based at Buturlinovka. The 899th Regiment was formed in 1993, receiving personnel and aircraft from other disbanded units, but formally assumed the traditions of the 3rd Corps Aviation Detachment of the Imperial Russian Army, formed on 18 June 1914 in Lida, making it the oldest air unit in Russia. In 2014 Viktor Bondaryev, then the commander-in-chief of the VVS and previously commander of the 899 ShAP, announced that the attack regiment at Buturlinovka would be re-created in 2017, when the Su-34s left the base. However, restoration of the 899 ShAP has been postponed for the time being.

159th Fighter Aviation Regiment (159 IAP)

Location: Besovets (Petrozavodsk)
Commanding officer: Colonel Aleksey Shatalov

This regiment was formed in 1940. From the end of World War II until 1992 it was based in Poland; it has been operating the Su-27 family since 1987. In 2009–10 the regiment was transformed, first into the 6961 AvB and then into the 2 AvGr 7000 AvB, being added to with airworthy Su-27s from the disbanded 9 IAP (Kilp-Yavr) and 177 IAP (Lodeynoye Pole). In 2013 the unit was transformed again into the 159 IAP; the regiment carries the Guard title.

Renewal of the regiment's equipment began at the end of 2015 and beginning of 2016 with a few (reportedly seven) upgraded Su-27SM fighters, transferred to Besovets from Dzyomgi and Tsentralnaya Uglovaya air bases in the Far East, both then re-equipping with new Su-35S fighters. A year later, on 6 December 2016, the initial four Su-35S fighters arrived in Besovets, too.

As of end of 2018 the regiment had two complete Su-35S squadrons; the third squadron operates Su-27SM fighters.

A long-term 'Flanker' operator, the 159th Fighter Aviation Regiment today flies the latest Su-35S from Besovets. This example, with wingtip R-73 missiles, is RF-81746 '58 Red'. (Piotr Butowski)

During 2013–15 a minor reconstruction of the base was carried out. The runway surface was partially replaced; the subsurface drainage, treatment facilities, electrical power supply, illumination and communication devices were modernised. Aircraft parking places and taxiways were enlarged. Since it is also the civil airport of Petrozavodsk, civil navigation equipment is being installed under a second stage of work, and the terminal is being modernised. The runway is 2,500m (8,202ft) long and 46m (151ft) wide.

790th Fighter Aviation Regiment (790 IAP)
Location: Khotilovo

The 790 IAP has been operating MiG-31 interceptors since 1994. In 2009 the regiment was transformed into the 6968 AvB, and a year later into the 4th Aviation Group of the 7000 AvB. In September 2009 a Su-27 squadron from the disbanded 611 IAP (Dorokhovo) was added to the two MiG-31 squadrons. Eventually, in 2013, the unit regained its traditional name 790 IAP. The regimental day is 15 May, commemorating the date in 1942 when the regiment first entered combat.

In 2014 the regiment began to obtain upgraded MiG-31BM interceptors and then upgraded Su-27SM fighters, transferred from Far East-based regiments. Currently there are two MiG-31BM squadrons and two dozen Su-27 and Su-27SMs (probably only half of these are active). Since December 2018 the squadron has been receiving Su-35S fighters to replace the Su-27s, which in turn are being handed over to the Naval Aviation of the Baltic Fleet. The runway is 3,000m (9,843ft) long and 45m (148ft) wide.

4th Independent Reconnaissance Aviation Squadron (4 ORAE)
Location: Shatalovo

Until 2009, the renowned 47 ORAP was based at Shatalovo with one squadron of 12 Su-24MR and one squadron of 12 MiG-25RB aircraft (plus five MiG-25U trainers). In 1971 and 1973 several MiG-25R aircraft of the 47 ORAP deployed to Egypt and flew reconnaissance missions over Israel. In 2009, the 47 ORAP was disbanded and the few airworthy aircraft (one Su-24MR squadron and a MiG-25RB flight) were transferred to Voronezh, where they became part of the 7000 AvB. Shatalovo air base was left vacant for several years.

Quite unexpectedly, in 2014 a decision was made to restore the Shatalovo unit, in reduced form, as the 4 ORAE. The squadron was formally established on 31 December 2014; renovation of the runway and taxiways continued for many months after (the runway at Shatalovo measures 2,500 × 60m; 8,202 × 197ft). Aircraft began to arrive beginning in October 2015 – a Su-24MR squadron and an An-30 detachment, which returned from Voronezh. The enlargement of the unit to regiment size is planned in future; it is also scheduled to obtain a squadron of new Su-34s. It is not known what number the regiment will be given after restoration, since its traditional number 47 has already been passed on to Voronezh's 47 SAP regiment.

33rd Independent Transport Composite Aviation Regiment (33 OTSAP)
Location: Levashovo (St Petersburg)

This is a typical specialist transport regiment, serving the HQ of the Western MD and the 6th Army. It operates a dozen An-26 aircraft, several An-12s and An-72s, single An-148s and Tu-134s, as well as a squadron of Mi-8 transport helicopters. The regiment's new

Take-off by An-12 RF-12561 '16 Red', assigned to the 33rd Independent Transport Composite Aviation Regiment at Levashovo, outside St Petersburg. (Piotr Butowski)

The all-new 15th Army Aviation Brigade at Ostrov is now a major centre of army aviation, and includes Ka-52 RF-91336 '44 White' **(above left)** and Mi-28N RF-95326 '03 White'. (both Piotr Butowski)

acquisitions comprise three An-148-100 aircraft, delivered in 2014–17. Levashovo airfield, situated virtually on the outskirts of St Petersburg, has a runway 2,720m (8,924ft) long and 42m (138ft) wide. A duty post at Gromovo airfield, 70km (44 miles) further north, is subordinated to the regiment. The An-26 that crashed on approach to landing at Hmeimim air base in Syria, killing six crewmembers and 33 passengers on 6 March 2018, belonged to the 33 OTSAP.

15th Army Aviation Brigade (15 Br AA)

Location: Ostrov
Commanding officer: Colonel Igor Chekmizov

This is a totally new formation without any historical traditions. It was formed in 2013 at Ostrov air base, where the naval aviation crew conversion centre had been based until 2009. Since mid-2013 the brigade has been receiving Mi-28N and Mi-35M helicopters, plus Ka-52s since 2014. Currently the brigade has a squadron of 12 Mi-28N and four Mi-35M attack helicopters, a squadron of 16 Mi-8MTV-5 assault helicopters, a squadron of 12 Ka-52 attack helicopters and a detachment of four Mi-26 heavy transport helicopters. The brigade also operates Mi-8MTPR-1 Rychag electronic warfare helicopters.

332nd Independent Helicopter Regiment (332 OVP)

Location: Pushkin, Pribylovo

The present 332 OVP is a merger of two helicopter units based near St Petersburg. In the past, the 332 OVP with a Mi-24 squadron (including upgraded Mi-24PN) and a Mi-8 squadron was based at Pribylovo; the 147th Independent Electronic Warfare Helicopter Squadron with several Mi-8PPA and Mi-8SMV rotorcraft was based at Pushkin. In December 2010 these and some other smaller units were transformed into the 549 AvB AA and on 1 December 2016 the base became the 332 OVP. The regimental HQ is located in Pushkin; the aviation group is based at Pribylovo airfield. Currently the 332

Above left: The 332nd Independent Helicopter Regiment at Pushkin operates this Mi-35M, RF-13028 '52 Red', equipped with the Vitebsk self-defence suite. (Piotr Butowski)

Above right: The Vyazma-based 440th Independent Helicopter Regiment includes Ka-52 RF-90392 '80 Red'. (Piotr Butowski)

OVP has one Mi-8 squadron (including new Mi-8MTV-5 and electronic warfare variants), one Mi-28N and Mi-35M squadron based at Pushkin, and a Mi-8 squadron plus a few old Mi-24PNs based at Pribylovo.

440th Independent Helicopter Regiment (440 OVP)

Location: Vyazma
Commanding officer: Colonel Rafael Salikov

The 440th Regiment with Mi-8 and Mi-24 helicopters (including K and R special purpose versions) was formed in 1987 in East Germany. In July 1992 the regiment was withdrawn to Vyazma, where the Germans built a housing facility for the unit's personnel. In 2009 the regiment was transformed into the 6996 AvB (along with reinforcement by Mi-24 helicopters from the disbanded 45 OVP based at Oreshkovo) and in 2011 it became the 378 AvB AA. On 1 December 2017 the base was transformed again into the 440 OVP.

Until 2014 the base operated old Mi-24 and Mi-8 versions, with one squadron of each type. Re-equipment began in 2014, when Mi-28Ns and then Mi-8MTV-5s arrived; in March 2018 the regiment received an initial eight Ka-52 helicopters. As of autumn 2018 the regiment had around 20 Mi-24 and Mi-28N helicopters, approximately 20 Mi-8s (including Mi-8MTPR, Mi-8SMV and other electronic warfare versions) as well as around 10 Ka-52 helicopters. Several dozen non-airworthy Mi-8s and Mi-24s are stored on the airfield periphery. The Rus' aerobatic team flying L-39C aircraft is also based at the same Vyazma airfield.

Aviation units assigned to the Western Military District/6th Air Force and Air Defence Army

Formation	Unit	Location	Inventory
105 SAD		Voronezh	
	14 IAP	Khalino (Kursk)	Su-30SM (2 sqn)
	47 SAP	Buturlinovka (planned Voronezh)	Su-34 (2 sqn)
	159 IAP	Besovets (Petrozavodsk)	Su-27SM (1 sqn), Su-35S (2 sqn)
	790 IAP	Khotilovo	MiG-31BM (2 sqn), Su-27SM/Su-35S (1 sqn)
	4 ORAE	Shatalovo	Su-24MR (1 sqn), An-30 (1 det)
33 OTSAP		Levashovo (St Petersburg)	Special transports
15 Br AA		Ostrov	Ka-52 (1 sqn), Mi-8MTV-5/Mi-8MTPR-1 (1 sqn), Mi-28N/Mi-35M (1 sqn), Mi-26 (1 det)
332 OVP		Pushkin	Mi-8, including EW versions (1 sqn), Mi-28N/Mi-35M (1 sqn)
		Pribylovo	Mi-28N/Mi-24 (1 sqn)
440 OVP		Vyazma	Ka-52 (1 sqn), Mi-8MTV-5/MTPR/SMV/PPA (1 sqn), Mi-8/Mi-24 (1 sqn)

Military District HQ

I St Petersburg

VVS Bases

1 Ostrov
2 Pribylovo
3 Levashovo (St Petersburg)
4 Pushkin
5 Besovets (Petrozavodsk)
6 Khotilovo
7 Vyazma
8 Shatalovo
9 Khalino (Kursk)
10 Voronezh
11 Buturlinovka

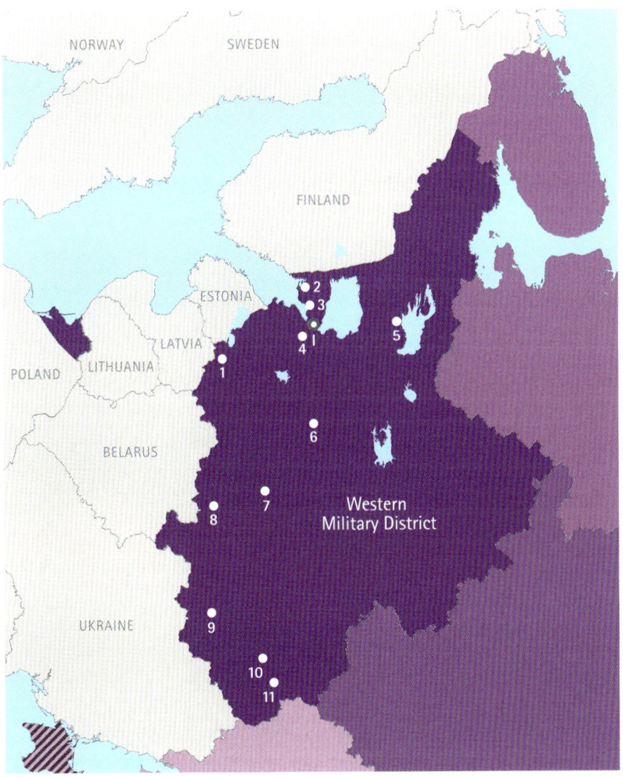

Key

Military District HQ

VVS Base

occupied territory

A map of the Western Military District and the 6th Air Force and Air Defence Army. (Map by James Lawrence)

11th Air Force and Air Defence Army (11 A VVS PVO)

HQ: Khabarovsk
Commanding officer: Major General Vladimir Kravchenko

11 August 1941, when the HQ of the Far Eastern Air Defence Zone was established in Khabarovsk, is considered the day of establishment of the 11th Army. On 1 March 2009 the army was transformed into the 3rd AF and AD Command and on 1 August 2015 it became the 11th Army. During the reform of 2009–10 the 14th AF and AD Army at Novosibirsk was disbanded, and its units were divided among its neighbours; the eastern part, concentrated around Chita, was taken over by the present-day 11th Army. The 11 A VVS PVO is subordinated to the Joint Strategic Command of the Eastern Military District. The 11th Army has been decorated with the Red Banner order.

The air units of 11th Army are concentrated around two centres, Khabarovsk in the east and Chita in the west; the distance between them is 1,600km (994 miles). Combat aircraft in the east are organised into the 303rd Composite Aviation Division with its HQ in Khurba. In the west, near Chita, there are for the time being two independent combat aircraft regiments, the fighter 120 OIAP in Domna and the attack 266 OShAP in Step' (temporarily in Domna).

Plans for 2019 announced by the defence minister Sergey Shoygu on 27 February provide for the creation of an HQ for another composite aviation division in Chita, which would joint these regiments, and possibly a new Su-34 regiment in Dzhida.

Apart from the air units, the 11th Army includes three SAM divisions: the 93rd AD Division with its HQ in Vladivostok and two regiments in Vladivostok (S-400, S-300V, Pantsir-S) and in Nakhodka (S-400, Pantsir-S), the 25th AD Division with its HQ in

An unarmed MiG-31BM from the historic 22nd Fighter Aviation Regiment scrambles from its Tsentralnaya Uglovaya base. (Russian MoD)

Komsomolsk-on-Amur, and three regiments in Khabarovsk (S-300PS), Bolshaya Kartel (S-300PM) and Birobidzhan (S-300V), plus the 26th AD Division in Chita with one missile regiment in Chita (S-300PS).

303rd Composite Aviation Division (303 SAD)

HQ: Khurba (Komsomolsk on Amur)
Commanding officer: Major General Alexander Putilov

This division first entered combat on 22 February 1943; this is the divisional day. On 1 December 2009 the 303rd Division was disbanded. It was re-created a year later, on 1 December 2010 as the 6983rd Aviation Base (1st Grade) with its HQ in Khurba. Finally, on 1 December 2013, it was transformed again into the 303 SAD and its aviation groups became regiments once again. In 2010 the division took over the traditions from the 18 ShAP: the Guard and Vitebsk titles and the orders of Red Banner (awarded twice), Suvorov and French Legion of Honour.

18th Attack Aviation Regiment (18 ShAP)

Location: Chernigovka
Commanding officer: Colonel Yuri Plaksin

This regiment was formed in 1938. Between May and July 1943, a squadron of French pilots were incoporated, and later detached as the independent Normandie-Niemen Regiment. To commemorate these events, the 18 ShAP was named Normandie-Niemen on 9 May 1995. In 1993 the regiment was equipped with Su-25 attack aircraft and on 9 November 2009 the 18 ShAP was disbanded.

On 1 December 2009 the 6983 AvB (from December 2010 the 7th Aviation Group of the 6983 AvB) was formed of personnel and equipment from several disbanded units (18 ShAP, 187 ShAP and 319 OVP), at Chernigovka air base, with two Su-25 squadrons and two helicopter squadrons. Finally, on 23 October 2013, the 18 ShAP was formed again from the base's attack aircraft (23 October is now the regimental day). Amid this upheaval the regiment lost its traditions; in December 2013 only the name Normandie-Niemen was restored.

The regiment currently has two squadrons of Su-25SM and UB attack aircraft. The runway of Chernigovka air base is 2,500m (8,202ft) long and 45m (148ft) wide. The regiment maintains a duty post at Vozdvizhenka airfield.

22nd Fighter Aviation Regiment (22 IAP)

Location: Tsentralnaya Uglovaya (Vladivostok)
Commanding officer: Colonel Sergey Bardin

This regiment's traditions date back to 1918; since 1934 the unit has been based at its current location near Vladivostok. Since 1995 the regiment has operated the Su-27 and it began to receive Su-27SM fighters in December 2007. On 30 January 2009 the 22 IAP was transformed into the 6989 AvB, and then into the 4 AvGr 6983 AvB. In 2009,

Carrying mission markings denoting operations in Syria, Su-35S RF-95816 '24 Red' (formerly '06 Red') is on strength with the 23rd Fighter Aviation Regiment at Dzyomgi. (Piotr Butowski)

the unit received a squadron of MiG-31 interceptors from the disbanded 530 IAP at Chuguyevka. In December 2013 the unit was transformed again into the 22 IAP; in the process, the regiment lost its historic traditions. The regimental day is 6 December. The base runway is 2,500m (8,202ft) long and 60m (197ft) wide.

Beginning in 2014 the 22 IAP transferred its Su-27SMs to other regiments, and beginning in July 2015 it received a squadron of new Su-35S fighters. Since December 2015 the regiment has also been receiving upgraded MiG-31BM interceptors from the Nizhny Novgorod facility.

Currently the regiment has one Su-35S squadron (with a handful of Su-30M2 two-seaters for training) and two MiG-31BM squadrons, as well as a dozen or so non-airworthy MiG-31s without upgrade.

Re-creation of the Chuguyevka regiment

Until 2009, the 530 IAP with MiG-31 interceptors was based at Chuguyevka (Sokolovka) air base; it was from this unit that Lt Viktor Belenko defected to Japan with his MiG-25P on 6 September 1976. The base is kept in readiness as a reserve airfield for the 22 IAP. Along with the arrival of further upgraded MiG-31BM and new Su-35S fighters for the 22 IAP, it is expected the MiG-31BMs will be detached to form a new regiment, probably based at Chuguyevka.

The 277th Bomber Aviation Regiment located at Khurba has flown the Su-24 series since the mid-1970s. Su-24M2 RF-95103 '72 White' was photographed in May 2015.
(Russian MoD)

23rd Fighter Aviation Regiment (23 IAP)
Location: Dzyomgi (Komsomolsk on Amur)

The 60 IAP was formed in 1939 at Dzyomgi airfield (which in the local Nanai language means 'birch grove'), where it has been based ever since. In 1985 it was the first unit equipped with new Su-27 fighters (Dzyomgi is also the factory airfield for Sukhoi's KnAAZ, manufacturer of the Su-27, Su-35 and Su-57). In December 2000 the 60 IAP was transformed into the 23 IAP, receiving personnel and Su-27s from the disbanded 404 IAP (Orlovka). In December 2009 the 23 IAP was transformed into the 6987 AvB, and in December 2010 into the 5th Aviation Group of the 6983 AvB. Finally, in December 2013, it became the 23 IAP again. In January 2018 the regiment regained the title Tallinn, lost during the turbulence of reorganisation.

On 23 December 2004 the 23 IAP accepted the initial seven upgraded Su-27SM fighters; in summer 2006 it already had two squadrons. In February 2014 the regiment received a squadron of 12 Su-35S fighters and passed the Su-27SMs to other units. Currently the 23 IAP has two Su-35S squadrons and a small number of Su-30SM two-seaters for training. The base has a runway 2,480m (8,136ft) long and 80m (262ft) wide.

On 3 August 2018 a flight of Su-35S fighters from the 23 IAP was permanently deployed (the aircraft and crews rotate every month) to Yasnyi airfield on the island of Iturup (Etorofu) in the Kuril Islands archipelago. These additional forces are deployed on the Kurils to strengthen Moscow's position in negotiations with Japan about the related peace treaty and future status of these islands. The 23 IAP also maintains a duty post at Sokol airfield on Sakhalin.

Su-24MR RF-95057 '07 Yellow' of the 3rd Independent Reconnaissance Aviation Squadron at Varfolomeyevka was intercepted over the Sea of Japan on 16 January 2019. (Japan MoD)

277th Bomber Aviation Regiment (277 BAP)
Location: Khurba (Komsomolsk on Amur)
Commanding officer: Colonel Denis Merkulov

This regiment was formed on 13 September 1941 and in October 1970, after the Sino-Soviet border conflict, it was deployed to Khurba, 300km (186 miles) away from the Chinese border (Khurba in the local Nanai language means 'semi-dugout'). On 1 December 2009 the 277 BAP was transformed into the 6988 AvB, and a year later into the 2 AvGr 6983 AvB; in 2013 the regiment returned to its former name. During the reorganisation of 2010 the regiment lost its title Mława; this was restored by presidential decree in January 2018. The regimental day is 13 September.

Since 1975 the regiment had operated Su-24 bombers; in 2009 it accepted Su-24M2 aircraft from the disbanded 302 BAP (Pereyaslavka). In 2016–17 the 277 BAP received its full complement of two squadrons of Su-34s (the first received on 31 May 2016).

Currently the regiment has two Su-34 squadrons and one Su-24M2 squadron. Khurba air base has the runway 2,500m (8,202ft) long and 40m (131ft) wide.

3rd Independent Reconnaissance Aviation Squadron (3 ORAE)
Location: Varfolomeyevka
Commanding officer: Lieutenant Colonel Sergey Nomokonov

Until 2009 this was the 799 ORAP, a regiment equipped with Su-24MR aircraft; in 2009 it was transformed into the 6985 AvB, and in 2010 it became the3 AvGr 6983 AvB. In 2013 the unit was transformed into an independent reconnaissance squadron, the 3 ORAE.

The runway of Varfolomeyevka air base is 2,500m (8,202ft) long and 42m (138ft) wide. Apart from a squadron of airworthy Su-24MRs, there are around 20 unserviceable aircraft at the base.

120th Independent Fighter Aviation Regiment (120 OIAP)

Location: Domna
Commanding officer: Colonel Sergey Trunin

This regiment was formed in 1969 as the 120 IAP, located in Belarus, but it was never to be based there permanently; this was a period of tension between the USSR and China and new units were hastily formed to reinforce the border. In August 1969 the 120 IAP with MiG-21S fighters was deployed to Domna air base near Chita, where it has been based ever since. In early 1993 the regiment was equipped with MiG-29s from the disbanded 176 IAP (Mikha Tskhakaya, Georgia). In 2009 the 120 IAP was transformed into the 6982 AvB and on 1 December 2010 it was incorporated into the new 412th Aviation Base, with two MiG-29 squadrons from the former 120 IAP, two Su-25 squadrons from the former 266 ShAP and two Mi-8 and Mi-24 squadrons from the former 112 OVP. In 2013 the helicopters were detached as an independent unit (see below, 112 OVP) in Chita, and the 120 OSAP was formed at Domna with Su-25 and MiG-29 aircraft. In 2015 the Su-25s were detached as the re-created 226 OShAP (see below) and the 120th regiment once again became a fighter regiment, the 120 OIAP. Currently the 120 OIAP has two Su-30SM squadrons; in November 2013 it became the first operational unit to receive Su-30SMs. The regimental day is 3 July.

266th Independent Attack Aviation Regiment (266 OShAP)

Location: Domna (planned Step' Olovyannaya)

This regiment was formed in 1941. In 1969 it was deployed to the proximity of China, to Nalaykha air base in Mongolia, and in 1989 moved to Step' air base in Olovyannaya. In the early 1990s it was equipped with Su-25 attack aircraft and renamed the 266 ShAP. On 1 December 2009 the regiment was transformed into the 2 AvGr 6980 AvB, and in

Su-30SM '29 Red' taxies at Domna in May 2015. The operating unit is the 120th Independent Fighter Aviation Regiment, the first operational unit to receive this variant of the 'Flanker'. (Russian MoD)

2010 deployed to Domna where it was incorporated into the new 412th Aviation Base; Step' air base was closed down. In 2013 the base was transformed into the 120 OSAP.

On 1 December 2015 the Su-25s were detached as the re-created 266 OShAP with the intention of deploying it to Step'. In January 2014 a thorough reconstruction of Step' airfield began, and was due to be completed by 2016. However, the work was abandoned halfway through and nothing has changed at this airfield for several years. The end of work was announced for 2019, but seems unlikely. After the reconstruction, two Su-25 squadrons (24 aircraft), plus a UAV squadron (four long-range and four medium-range systems, probably the Orion and Forpost) are to be based at Step'.

New Su-34 regiment

On 20 August 2018, in a local TV report from Domna air base, one of the pilots said that 'soon the Su-34 new-generation aircraft will arrive at the base'. Two variants are possible. The Su-34s may be used to form a new bomber regiment, probably based at Dzhida, where the 2 BAP's Su-24M bombers was based until 2010; the airfield remains in fairly good condition. It is also possible that the Su-34s will be delivered to the 266th Regiment, to replace the Su-25s. The re-equipment of the 266 OShAP with unspecified new aircraft was announced as early as 2015.

35th Independent Transport Composite Aviation Regiment (35 OTSAP)

Location: Khabarovsk Tsentralnyi

This is a unit equipped with special-use transport aircraft, serving the HQ of the Eastern Military District and the 11th Army. The regiment has a dozen or so aircraft, half of which are An-26s, plus several An-12s, Tu-134s and Tu-154s. The regimental day is 12 September. The runway at Khabarovsk Tsentralny airfield is 2,400m (7,874ft) long and 36m (118ft) wide.

The 18 Br AA, an aviation group of the FSB, and an air rescue group of the Ministry of Emergency Situations are based at the same airfield.

18th Brigade of Army Aviation (18 Br AA)

Location: Khabarovsk Tsentralnyi

The 18 Br AA was formed on 1 December 2016 from the 573 AvB AA, which in turn was the successor to the 825th Helicopter Regiment (at Garovka near Khabarovsk) that was disbanded in 2009. In recent years the unit's equipment has been modernised: in 2013 older Mi-8 versions were replaced by the new Mi-8AMTSh; Ka-52 combat helicopters arrived during 2014–15. The brigade currently has one squadron with 18 Mi-8AMTSh helicopters, one squadron with 18 Ka-52 attack helicopters and one squadron with six heavy-lift Mi-26s and several Mi-8s, including Mi-8SMV electronic warfare versions.

The brigade also maintains a detachment of Mi-8s on the island of Iturup (Etorofu) in the Kuril Islands. Apparently one helicopter squadron is still lacking to obtain the full complement of an army aviation brigade.

112th Independent Helicopter Regiment (112 OVP)

Location: Chita Cheryomushki (Chita Northwest)

This regiment's history begins in 1966; in July 1967 it was deployed, like many other units, to Nerchinsk, 250km (155 miles) away from the border with China. In March 1969 the regiment participated in the battle for Damansky Island on the Ussuri River. Since 2003 it has been based at Cheryomushki airfield in Chita.

In 2009 the regiment was transformed into the 320th Aviation Base; a squadron of An-12, An-26 and other transport aircraft based at the same airfield (former 36 OSAP) were also assigned to the base. On 1 December 2010 the 320 AvB was incorporated as an aviation group within the large 412 AvB with its HQ at Domna. In 2013 the helicopters in Chita regained independence, first as the 439 AvB AA and, since December 2016, as the 112 OVP.

Currently the regiment has two squadrons of Mi-8AMTSh transport helicopters and a squadron of Mi-24P attack helicopters; replacement of the Mi-24Ps with new Mi-28NMs is planned.

There are also more than 80 non-airworthy helicopters (without rotor blades), including 60 Mi-24s and more than 20 Mi-8s at the base.

A member of the Chernigovka ground crew marshalls Ka-52 RF-90658 '23 Yellow', in service with the resident 319th Independent Helicopter Regiment. (Russian MoD)

Another type in service with the 319th Independent Helicopter Regiment at Chernigovka is the Mi-8AMTSh combat transport, including RF-91180 '59 Yellow', nearest camera. (Russian MoD)

319th Independent Helicopter Regiment (319 OVP)

Location: Chernigovka

This regiment is considered the successor to one of the first aviation groups established by Vladimir Lenin in 1918, and during the Soviet era it even was named after Lenin. In 1960 the unit was transformed into a helicopter regiment, the 319 OVP. In 1971 it was the first unit to re-equip with Mi-24 attack helicopters (Chernigovka is 60km, 37 miles away from Arsenyev, where Mi-24s were manufactured). In 2009 the regiment became a part of the 6983 AvB, a year later it became the 575 AvB AA, and on 1 December 2016 it was transformed again into a regiment with the historic number 319. The regiment currently has a squadron of Mi-8AMTSh transport helicopters, a squadron of Ka-52 attack helicopters and a handful of Mi-26 helicopters. The regimental day is 5 December.

VKS aviation units assigned to the Eastern Military District/11th Air Force and Air Defence Army

Formation	Unit	HQ/Location	Inventory
303 SAD		Khurba (Komsomolsk on Amur)	
	18 ShAP	Chernigovka	Su-25SM (2 sqn)
	22 IAP	Tsentralnaya Uglovaya (Vladivostok)	MiG-31BM (2 sqn), Su-35S/Su-30M2 (1 sqn)
	23 IAP	Dzyomgi (Komsomolsk on Amur)	Su-35S/Su-30SM (2 sqn)
	277 BAP	Khurba (Komsomolsk on Amur)	Su-24M2 (1 sqn), Su-34 (2 sqn)
	3 ORAE	Varfolomeyevka	Su-24MR (1 sqn)
120 OIAP		Domna	Su-30SM (2 sqn)
266 OShAP		Domna (planned Step' Olovyannaya)	Su-25SM (2 sqn)
35 OTSAP		Khabarovsk Tsentralnyi	Special transports
18 Br AA		Khabarovsk Tsentralnyi	Ka-52 (1 sqn), Mi-8AMTSh (1 sqn), Mi-8/Mi-8SMV/Mi-26 (1 sqn)
112 OVP		Chita Cheryomushki	Mi-8AMTSh (2 sqn), Mi-24P (1 sqn)
319 OVP		Chernigovka	Ka-52 (1 sqn), Mi-8AMTSh (1 sqn), Mi-26 (1 det)

Military District HQ

I Khabarovsk

VVS Bases

1 Domna
2 Chita Cheryomushki
3 Step'
4 Khurba (Komsomolsk on Amur)
5 Dzyomgi (Komsomolsk on Amur)
6 Chernigovka
7 Varfolomeyevka
8 Tsentralnaya Uglovaya (Vladivostok)
9 Iturup
10 Khabarovsk Tsentralnyi

Key

Military District HQ
VVS Base

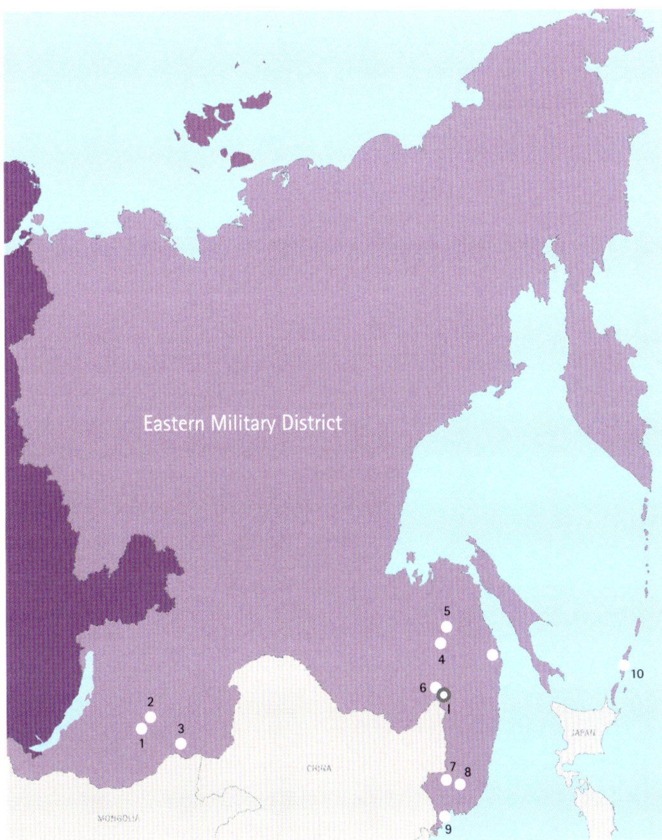

A map of the Eastern Military District and the 11th Air Force and Air Defence Army. (Map by James Lawrence)

14th Air Force and Air Defence Army (14 A VVS PVO)

HQ: Yekaterinburg
Commanding officer: Lieutenant General Alexander Tatarenko
Deputy Commander, Chief of Aviation: Oleg Solovyov

The predecessor of the 14th Army is the Novosibirsk Air Defence District, established on 1 July 1952. In 2009 the 14th Army was transformed into the 2nd AF and AD Command, being joined by some units from the disbanded 5th AF and AD Army with its HQ in Yekaterinburg. On 1 August 2015 the 2nd Command was transformed again into the 14th Army. The 14 A VVS PVO is subordinated to the Joint Strategic Command of the Central Military District.

This is the smallest of all the air armies in Russia in terms of number of units, although the Central MD occupies the largest area of all – seven million square kilometres (2,702,715 square miles), i.e. 41 per cent of the territory of Russia (the Eastern MD is only slightly smaller). The fixed-wing aircraft component comprises two regiments of MiG-31 interceptors and one composite regiment of Su-34, Su-24M and Su-24MR aircraft. The helicopter component of the 14th Army is also fairly limited; it comprises one brigade and one regiment, both of reduced strength.

On 1 April 2011 the 14th Army (then as the 2nd Command) took over eight former independent helicopter squadrons from the Strategic Rocket Troops, which were incorporated into two army aviation bases. Two foreign Russian air bases in Kyrgyzstan and Tajikistan are also subordinated into the 14th AF and AD Army.

Apart from the air units, the 14th Army also comprises the 41st AD Division with its HQ in the town of Ob with three SAM regiments in Novosibirsk (S-400, S-300PS), Angarsk (S-300PM) and Achinsk (S-300PS), and the 76th AD Division with its HQ in Samara with three missile regiments in Engels (S-300PS), Yekaterinburg (S-300PS) and Samara (S-300PS).

21st Composite Aviation Division (21 SAD)

HQ: Chelyabinsk
Commanding officer: Major General Vladimir Koryagin

Until 2009 the HQ of the 21 SAD was located in Dzhida, near Baikal. Later it was transformed into the 6980th Aviation Base (1st Grade) with the HQ moved to Chelyabinsk, and in 2015 the previous 21 SAD name was restored.

2nd Composite Aviation Regiment (2 SAP)

Location: Shagol (Chelyabinsk)
Commanding officer: Colonel Andrey Yermakov

This regiment's history dates back to 14 May 1938. In August 1969 it was deployed to the Far East of the USSR, to Dzhida. In 2010 Dzhida air base was closed down and the 21 BAP disbanded. Two Su-24M squadrons were moved from Dzhida to Shagol airfield in Chelyabinsk, where they were merged with a squadron of Su-24MR reconnaissance aircraft from the disbanded 313 ORAP (Bada), creating an aviation group of the 6980 AvB.

In 2015 the group was again transformed into a regiment, the 2 SAP. For participation in combat operations in Syria, the regiment was awarded the Suvorov Order in February 2019.

In November 2017 the pilots of the 2 SAP began conversion to the Su-34 fighter-bomber in Lipetsk. In September 2018 the first Su-34s arrived in Chelyabinsk. Currently the regiment has one full squadron of Su-34s, one squadron under conversion from Su-24M to Su-34 (the first four Su-34s for the squadron arrived in December 2018; conversion is planned to be accomplished in 2019) and one squadron of Su-24MRs.

In 2018 it was announced that the regiment had received an 'upgraded Su-24MR reconnaissance aircraft'; the extent of the upgrade is unknown. The runway at Chelyabinsk is 2,550m (8,366ft) long and 41m (135ft) wide.

712th Fighter Aviation Regiment (712 IAP)

Location: Kansk
Commanding officer: Colonel Yevgeny Averyanov

This unit was formed on 27 June 1938; since July 1959 it has been based at Kansk, Siberia. On 1 June 2009 the 712 IAP was transformed into the 6979 AvB, in November 2010 it became the 3 AvGr 6980 AvB, and on 1 December 2015 the previous 712 IAP name was restored.

In May 1993 the regiment received its first MiG-31B aircraft from the Nizhny Novgorod facility; later it also took over MiG-31 and MiG-31DZ aircraft from disbanded units.

Su-34 RF-81851 '07 Red' of the 2nd Composite Aviation Regiment after landing at Chelyabinsk. (Piotr Butowski)

In January 2011 MiG-31BMs that had undergone upgrade at the 514 ARZ repair facility in Rzhev arrived (Kansk was the first base to receive upgraded MiG-31BMs); since 2013 the unit has been operating a full complement of 24 MiG-31BMs. The runway at Kansk is 2,600m (8,530ft) long and 40m (131ft) wide.

A pair of MiG-31BM interceptors from Kansk is kept on permanent alert duty at Novosibirsk (Tolmachovo) airfield; the aircraft and crews rotate every month.

764th Fighter Aviation Regiment (764 IAP)

Location: Bolshoye Savino (Perm)
Commanding officer: Colonel Valery Khod'ko

This regiment was formed on 7 November 1952 at Bolshoye Savino airfield near Perm, where it has been based ever since; beginning in 1992 it has been operating MiG-31 interceptors. On 1 June 2009 the 764 IAP was transformed into the 6977 AvB, in November 2010 it became the 2 AvGr 6980 AvB, and on 1 December 2015 the previous 764 IAP name was restored.

Currently the regiment has two MiG-31 interceptor squadrons, successively upgraded to BM standard. The runway at Bolshoye Savino is 3,300m (10,827ft) long and 50m (164ft) wide.

32nd Independent Transport Composite Aviation Regiment (32 OTSAP)

Location: Koltsovo (Yekaterinburg)
Commanding officer: Colonel Andrey Kanarsky

This regiment serves the HQ of the Central Military District and the 14th AF and AD Army; it has around 20 fixed-wing aircraft and helicopters, including examples of the

An-72 RF-72917 '17 Red' is one of the 32nd Independent Transport Composite Aviation Regiment fleet at Yekaterinburg. (Piotr Butowski)

An-12, An-26, An-148, Tu-134 and Mi-8 at Koltsovo airport. A squadron from the regiment is deployed to Novosibirsk airfield (the former 37 OSAE). Another composite squadron with four Mi-8AMTSh-V helicopters and three An-26 transports was established in Kyzyl (Tuva) on 1 March 2019.

999th Aviation Base (999 AvB)

Location: Kant, Kyrgyzstan
Commanding officer: Colonel Andrey Yankin

Located in the municipality of Kant, 15km (9 miles) from Bishkek, the capital of Kyrgyzstan, the 999 AvB has a squadron of 12 Su-25M attack aircraft, two An-26 transport aircraft, two Mi-8 helicopters and four L-39C trainers (detached to the base by Kyrgyzstan). Reportedly, the base also operates Forpost UAVs. Initially, deployment of a flight of Su-27 fighters to the base was also planned, but the idea was later abandoned.

The Kant base was officially opened on 23 October 2003 as the air component of the Collective Rapid Reaction Force of the Collective Security Treaty Organisation (CSTO), a military alliance of Russia, Armenia, Belarus, Kazakhstan, Kyrgyzstan and Tajikistan.

214th (?) Aviation Group (214 [?] AvGr)

Location: Ayni (Dushanbe), Tajikistan

After the breakup of the USSR, the Soviet 201st Infantry Division remained in Tajikistan territory. In 2005 it was transformed into the 201st Military Base. In 2012 both nations signed an agreement stipulating that the Russian base will remain in Tajikistan territory until 2042.

Su-25SM RF-95132 '03 Blue' from the 999th Aviation Base in Kant received the name *Ismailbek Taranchiyev* in December 2017. (Russian MoD)

Mi-8MT RF-94949 '26 Yellow', from the 17th Brigade of Army Aviation at Kamensk Uralsky conducts a search and rescue drill in 2018. (Russian MoD)

The Russian contingent included a helicopter squadron (303 OVE) and an Su-25 attack aircraft group (670 AvGr), which on 1 January 2010 were merged into an aviation base with five Su-25 aircraft, four Mi-8 and four Mi-24 helicopters. In 2015 the base was transformed into an aviation group, possibly numbered 214; it comprised only helicopters. Currently, a squadron with 14–18 helicopters (half of them Mi-8s and half Mi-24s), four L-39 trainers and one Tu-134 passenger aircraft are based at Ayni (Gissar). The Su-25 attack aircraft arrive rarely (typically a flight of four aircraft), a few times a year; even more rarely, Su-24 tactical bombers may also be seen here.

17th Brigade of Army Aviation (17 Br AA)

Location: Kamensk Uralsky

The airfield at Kamensk Uralsky (also called Travyany after a neighbouring housing estate) had been vacant since 1998. The airfield was revived in December 2011, where the 48 AvB AA was formed there by gathering helicopters from disbanded units, including former squadrons of the Strategic Rocket Troops.

On 1 December 2018 the base was transformed into the 17th Army Aviation Brigade. The aviation group based at Uprun (Yuzhnouralsk) airfield, 230km (143 miles) south of Kamensk, is also part of the brigade.

In February 2017, 16 new Mi-8MTV-5 helicopters arrived in Kamensk to replace older Mi-8 versions. In December 2018 the brigade received around 20 Mi-24P attack

The 17th Brigade of Army Aviation maintains a squadron of Mi-26 heavy helicopters at Uprun. Among them is RF-36021 '04 Yellow'. (Russian MoD)

helicopters, for which a new squadron was formed. In February 2018 the Uprun group also received Mi-8MTV-5s.

Currently the 17 Br AA has one Mi-8MTV-5 squadron and one Mi-24P squadron at Kamensk Uralsky, and a squadron with Mi-8 and Mi-26 helicopters at Uprun airfield. The brigade's main is searching for landing spaceships and transport of astronauts after they have touched down in Kazakhstan or southern Ural.

337th Independent Helicopter Regiment (337 OVP)

Location: Tolmachovo (Novosibirsk)
Commanding officer: Colonel Sergey Barykin

The 337 OVP helicopter regiment was formed on 15 December 1978. During 2009–10 the regiment was transformed into the 562 AvB AA in several stages, being moved from Berdsk to Tolmachovo. In 2011 helicopters of several disbanded squadrons from the Strategic Rocket Troops were assigned to the base. On 1 December 2018 the base was transformed again into the 337 OVP.

The regiment has two squadrons, one equipped with Mi-8AMTSh-V and one with Mi-24P helicopters. Tolmachovo airfield, which is also the airport of Novosibirsk, has a runway 3,750m (12,303ft) long and 60m (197ft) wide; another runway, of similar dimensions, is rarely (if ever) used.

Mi-24P RF-91078 '06 Red' is a former 92nd Research Instructor Helicopter Squadron example from Klin. It arrived with the 17th Brigade of Army Aviation at Kamensk Uralsky in December 2018.
(Piotr Butowski)

Aviation units assigned to the Central Military District/14th Air Force and Air Defence Army

Formation	Unit	HQ/Location	Inventory
21 SAD		Chelyabinsk	
	2 SAP	Shagol (Chelyabinsk)	Su-24MR (1 sqn), Su34/Su-24M (1 sqn), Su-34 (1 sqn)
	712 IAP	Kansk	MiG-31BM (2 sqn)
	764 IAP	Bolshoye Savino (Perm)	MiG-31 (2 sqn)
32 OTSAP		Koltsovo (Yekaterinburg)	Special transports
999 AvB		Kant, Kyrgyzstan	Su-25SM (1 sqn), transports
214 (?) AvGr		Ayni (Dushanbe), Tajikistan	Mi-8/Mi-24 (1 sqn)
17 Br AA		Kamensk Uralsky	Mi-8MTV-5 (1 sqn), Mi-24P (1 sqn)
		Uprun	Mi-8MTV-5/Mi-26 (1 sqn)
337 OVP		Tolmachovo (Novosibirsk)	Mi-8AMTSh-V (1 sqn), Mi-24 (1 sqn)

Military District HQ

I Yekaterinburg

VVS Bases

1 Bolshoye Savino (Perm)
2 Kamensk Uralsky
3 Shagol (Chelyabinsk)
4 Uprun
5 Tolmachovo (Novosibirsk)
6 Kansk

Key

Military District HQ

VVS Base

A map of the Central Military District and the 14th Air Force and Air Defence Army. (Map by James Lawrence)

NAVAL AVIATION OF THE NAVY

Morskaya aviatsiya Voenno-morskogo flota (MA VMF)

HQ: Moscow
Chief of Naval Aviation (Nachalnik MA VMF): Major General Igor Kozhin
Manpower: 31,000 people

However awkward it sounds, the official name of the Russian naval aviation branch is the Naval Aviation of the Navy. The Russian Navy consists of four fleets – the Northern, Pacific, Baltic and Black Sea, plus a flotilla in the Caspian Sea. The fleets are managed by the Navy Main Staff in St Petersburg, although operationally each fleet is subordinated to one of the Joint Strategic Commands of the respective military districts. The Northern Fleet has a special position since it is the JSC of the Northern Fleet.

Naval aviation has been subject to serious degradation in the post-Soviet era. First of all, it lost its Tu-22M missile-carriers, which were tasked with combatting US aircraft carriers. The aircraft were gradually subject to attrition, until the remaining examples were finally transferred to the Russian Air Force in 2011.

The main mission of the anti-submarine warfare (ASW) aviation (Protivo-lodochnaya Aviatsiya, PLA) is to protect departing Russian submarines carrying intercontinental nuclear ballistic missiles against attacks by enemy submarines. In this role, the significance of the oceanic-range Tu-142 aircraft diminished and that of medium- and short-range Il-38 aircraft and Ka-27 ASW helicopters increased. The tasks of the Tu-142 are now shifting towards long-range patrol and reconnaissance. Only the 'big' fleets (Northern and Pacific) use Tu-142 and Il-38 ASW aircraft; the 'small' fleets (Baltic and Black Sea) only operate ASW helicopters. An extremely important task performed by naval aviation's Tu-142MR radio-relay aircraft is securing communications with commanders of submerged submarines carrying ballistic missiles.

Fighter-attack aviation (Istrebitelno-shturmovaya aviatsiya, ShA), with Su-24M strike aircraft, currently being replaced with Su-30SM multirole fighters, is for use against missile-carrying fast attack craft operating within the coastal zone. After many years of inactivity, the Ka-29 assault-transport helicopters are now returning to service. They are scheduled to be reinforced by Ka-52K carrier-based attack helicopters in future. The Su-24MR reconnaissance aircraft are gradually being retired and replaced by Forpost reconnaissance UAVs.

Most naval aviation aircraft are land-based; the only aircraft carrier is the *Admiral Kuznetsov*, assigned to the Northern Fleet and served by two shipborne fighter regiments based at Severomorsk, one with Su-33 and another with MiG-29K fighters. Shore-based fighters within naval aviation are the exception rather than the rule. In the Baltic Fleet there is a Su-27 regiment based at Chkalovsk; in the Northern Fleet, a MiG-31 squadron based at Monchegorsk; and in the Pacific Fleet, a MiG-31 squadron at Yelizovo. In all these cases their existence is purely accidental; the navy simply took over the air force units previously based at these locations.

Russian Naval Aviation is commanded from the **Central Command Post** (Tsentralnyi komandnyi punkt, TsKP) MA VMF in Moscow. Communications between the TsKP and air units is provided by the **Central Communications Node** (Tsentralnyi uzyel svyazi) MA VMF in Yam near Domodedovo, outside Moscow.

The Russian Naval Aviation Day is 17 July. On this day in 1916 four Russian M-9 flying boats reportedly shot down two German floatplanes over the Baltic Sea (however, there are serious doubts whether this engagement took place at all).

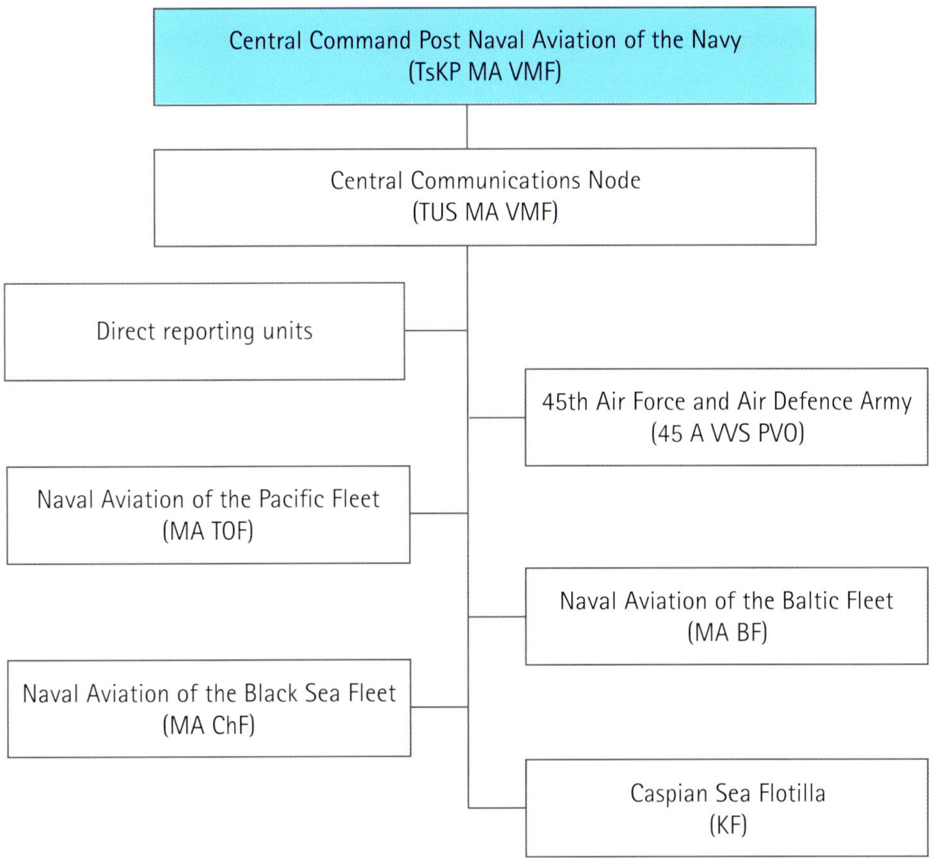

Command structure of the Naval Aviation of the Navy. (Harpia Publishing)

Il-38N RF-75355 '19 Yellow' from the 859th Combat Training and Flight Crew Conversion Centre of Naval Aviation at Yeysk and RF-75322 from '23 Yellow' from Nikolayevka, where it serves the Pacific Fleet. (Piotr Butowski)

Direct reporting units

859th Combat Training and Flight Crew Conversion Centre of Naval Aviation (859 TsBP PLS MA)

HQ: Yeysk
Commanding officer: Major General Aleksey Serdyuk

During the Soviet era the naval aviation training centre was the 33 TsBP PLS at Mykolayiv, Ukraine, succeeded after the breakup of the USSR by the 444 TsBP PLS at Ostrov near Pskov in Russia. On 1 December 1999 the 444th Centre in Ostrov was disbanded and the new 859th Training Centre in Yeysk was established. This organisation inherited its number from the 859th Naval Aviation Training Centre in Kacha, Crimea, leased from Ukraine and then disbanded in 2009 – it was here that foreign helicopter pilots were trained (for example, Chinese aircrews on the Ka-31). The day of the 859 TsBP PLS is commemorated on 1 July: it was on this date that the 859th Centre in Kacha was established, in 1981.

For carrier-based aircraft pilot training, an experimental facility was built at Saki, Crimea, in 1982. Colloquially known as Nitka (nazemnyi ispytatelno-trenirovochnyi komplex, ground-based research and training complex), this comprises a runway with a 'ski jump' ramp and arresting gear that replicates the deck of the *Admiral Kuznetsov* aircraft carrier.

The Nitka is still employed by Russian Naval Aviation, although it is only suited to limited use. In 2012 construction of a similar facility began in Yeysk; it was expected to be ready for use in 2018. The runway at Yeysk is 3,650m (11,975ft) long and 65m (213ft) wide.

Naval aviation aircrew training is conducted by 190th Training Composite Aviation Regiment (190 USAP) in Yeysk. The regiment has a small but diverse inventory, with one or two aircraft or helicopters of each type. These include the An-140-100, Il-38N, Ka-27, Ka-28, Ka-29, Mi-8, MiG-29KUBR, Su-25UTG, Su-30SM, Su-33 and Tu-142; it also has L-39C trainers.

The Aviation Squadron of Search and Rescue Providing (AEPSO), with An-12, An-26 and An-72 aircraft, is commanded by Colonel Yuri Kotlovenko and is also subordinated to the centre. The squadron is based at Ostafyevo (Shcherbinka) airfield near Moscow; the primary user of the airfield is Gazprom. The runway at Ostafyevo is 2,100m (6,890ft) long and 48m (157ft) wide.

Yeysk is home to this Ka-28 – the export version of the Ka-27PL. RF-19438 '34 Yellow' is operated by the resident 859th Combat Training and Flight Crew Conversion Centre of Naval Aviation. (Piotr Butowski)

Another 859th Combat Training and Flight Crew Conversion Centre of Naval Aviation asset is Ka-29 RF-34194 '38' Yellow. (Piotr Butowski)

A detailed ORBAT table of all MA VMF direct reporting units can be found on page 102.

45th Air Force and Air Defence Army (45 A VVS PVO)

HQ: Severomorsk
Commanding officer: Major General Alexander Otroshchenko
Deputy commander for aviation: Colonel Igor Matkovsky

The Northern Fleet with its HQ in Severomorsk is the most capable of all the Russian fleets; it operates in the Atlantic Ocean and all northern seas (including the Arctic Ocean). Its main strike force consists of eight submarines armed with intercontinental ballistic missiles, based in Gadzhiyevo near Murmansk. The only Russian aircraft carrier, *Admiral Kuznetsov*, is also assigned to the Northern Fleet.

The 45th AF and AD Army was formed in December 2015 from the Naval Aviation of the Northern Fleet. Apart from the air units, the 45th Army also comprises the 1st AD Division with its HQ in Severomorsk and four regiments of S-300, S-400 and Pantsir-S missiles. Another air defence division is being formed.

Unknown Shipborne Fighter Aviation Division (KIAD)

HQ: Severomorsk (?)

The HQ of this new division was probably established on 1 December 2018, but nothing more is known about it. Before December 2018 the 100th and 279th Regiments were both independent (OKIAP).

100th Shipborne Fighter Aviation Regiment (100 KIAP)

HQ: Severomorsk-3
Commanding officer: Colonel Vladimir Kokurin

The 100 KIAP regiment (until 1 December 2018 the independent 100 OKIAP) was formed on 1 December 2015 at Yeysk specifically to operate the new MiG-29KR/KUBR fighters. In 2017 the regiment was redeployed to its permanent base of Severomorsk-3. The runway at Severomorsk-3 is 2,500m (8,202ft) long and 60m (197ft) wide.

The regiment's name refers to the tradition of the former 100th Research and Training Regiment, formed in 1986 in Saki, Crimea to train pilots on the MiG-29K and Su-27K (Su-33) carrier-based fighters for the *Admiral Kuznetsov*, then under construction.

279th Shipborne Fighter Aviation Regiment (279 KIAP)

HQ: Severomorsk-3
Commanding officer: Colonel Pavel Podguzov

The 279 KIAP was formed in Saki, Crimea in December 1973 as the 279 OKShAP; it operated Yak-38 vertical take-off and landing aircraft. In summer 1976 it moved to Severomorsk-3 air base. The regiment currently has two incomplete squadrons of Su-33 fighters (14 aircraft in total); the third squadron has around seven Su-25UTG trainers and (since December 2016) two Su-30SM fighters, used as trainers in lieu of

The 100th Shipborne Fighter Aviation Regiment, now based at Severomorsk-3, was created specifically to operate the MiG-29KR/KUBR. This is MiG-29KR RF-92319 '43 Blue'. (Piotr Butowski)

the weary Su-27UBs. The unit's full name is 279th Smolensk, decorated with Red Banner order, Shipborne Fighter Aviation Regiment named after double Hero of the Soviet Union Boris Safonov.

98th Independent Composite Aviation Regiment (98 OSAP)

Location: Monchegorsk
Commanding officer: Colonel Alexander Prikhod'ko

This is former the 97th Reconnaissance Regiment of the Russian Air Force, to which the number and traditions of the famous 98 ORAP were passed in 1993. During 2009-10 it was initially the 6964 AvB, and then became the 3 AvGr 7000th AvB of the Air Force. In December 2013 the group was again transformed into a regiment, the 98 OSAP; in 2014 it was subordinated to the Russian Naval Aviation. The regimental day is 17 June.

The regiment is a 'composite' one: apart from its own Su-24MR reconnaissance aircraft, in 2009–10 it assumed responsibility for Su-24M bombers from the disbanded 67 BAP (Siversky) and MiG-31 interceptors from the 458 IAP (Kotlas).

Currently the regiment has one squadron of Su-24M, Su-24MR and MiG-31BM aircraft each; a dozen non-airworthy MiG-31s remain on the airfield periphery. The runway at Monchegorsk is 2,400m (7,874ft) long and 40m (131ft) wide.

7050th Aviation Base (7050 AvB)

HQ: Severomorsk-1

This base was formed in 2009 through the merger of the 403 OSAP operating Il-38 ASW aircraft and transport aircraft, the 830 OKPLVP operating Ka-27, Ka-29 and Mi-8 helicopters, and auxiliary units, all based at Severomorsk-1 (20km, 12 miles away from Severomorsk-3). Currently the 7050 AvB comprises a squadron of Il-38s (including upgraded Il-38Ns), a squadron of Ka-27 ASW helicopters (including upgraded Ka-27Ms), a squadron of Ka-27PS, Ka-29 and Mi-8 helicopters, and a SAR and transport squadron with An-26 aircraft and single An-12, Il-18 and Tu-134 aircraft.

Severomorsk-1 air base has been undergoing reconstruction since 2012. The runway has been lengthened from 3,000m (9,843ft) to 3,500m (11,483ft); it is 60m (197ft) wide. The taxiways, aircraft parking stands and other infrastructure have been built from scratch. Reconstruction of the airfield was halted in 2015–16, probably due to a lack of funding. Since the runway and one section of aircraft parking stands had been completed, the unfinished air base was reactivated in June 2018.

5th Independent ASW Aviation Squadron (5 OPLAE)

Location: Kipelovo (Fedotovo)
Commanding officer: Lieutenant Colonel Vasily Chernyshov

A Tu-142 squadron assigned to the 7050 AvB is based at Kipelovo (Fedotovo) airfield, 1,100km (684 miles) away from Severomorsk; during 2001–09 it had the number 73, while the latest reports indicate number 5 is correct. In 2009 the squadron was transformed into the 7051 AvB and in 2010 it was assigned to the 7050 AvB as an independent squadron. Currently the squadron has at least seven airworthy Tu-142MK and four Tu-142MR aircraft. Around eight more aircraft are awaiting overhaul; they are being successively returned to service by the Beriev facility in Taganrog. Kipelovo airfield has a runway 3,500m (11,483ft) long and 70m (230ft) wide.

Ka-27PS '55 Red' RF-19154 takes part in an air assault exercise on Chukotka in September 2018. The helicopter serves with the 7050 Aviation Base at Severomorsk-1. (Russian MoD)

The carrier-based Su-33 fighters are the responsibility of the 279th Shipborne Fighter Aviation Regiment at Severomorsk-3. (Piotr Butowski)

On 5 June 2016, one day after the US Navy's Harry S. Truman Carrier Strike Group launched its first strikes from the Mediterranean Sea over Syria and Iraq, Russia sent a Tu-142MK aircraft from Kipelovo to the same area in response; the aircraft was seen over Aleppo in Syria.

216th (?) Independent Unmanned Aerial Vehicles Regiment (216 [?] OP BLA)

Location: Severomorsk-1
Commanding officer: Colonel Andrey Baushev

This Forpost UAV regiment was formed in the Northern Fleet as an experiment; it is the first such unit in Russia. The next such units will be created in the Black Sea Fleet in Crimea and in the Pacific Fleet in Kamchatka. It commenced as a detachment with 20 personnel formed within the 7050th Aviation Base Severomorsk-1 in 2013; a year later it was expanded to squadron strength and in 2017 it became an independent regiment with 400 personnel. The regiment probably has the number 216.

In spring 2014 the squadron flew reconnaissance missions over Crimea with Forpost UAVs, during the annexation by Russia. In 2015, now stationed at Marinovka in Russia, it operated over Donbas in eastern Ukraine. Subsequently the unit conducted 'special missions' in Dagestan, Russia and in Syria.

The 7050 Aviation Base at Severomorsk-1 also operates transport aircraft, including a single An-12, '14 Yellow'. (Piotr Butowski)

Expanding borders: Arctic

Giving the Northern Fleet the status of a military district is related to Russian plans for expansion in the High Arctic, the region above the Arctic Circle. Within the Arctic, Russia seeks to gain access to new reserves of energy resources and make use of northern sea lanes (now easier to use thanks to the diminishing continental ice-sheet). The rights to the continental shelf below the Arctic are a subject of dispute between several nations. Expanding her military presence in the region, Russia gains additional arguments in this dispute.

For several years, former military bases have been restored or new facilities, including airfields, have been built in the Russian parts of the Arctic. Ultimately, Russia aims to have 13 military airfields in the region (confirmed in 2014 by the head of the National Defence Management Centre, Colonel General Mikhail Mizintsev). Some of these will have air units permanently based. Most of these reconstruction projects seem to have been significantly delayed due to a lack of funds, but they have not been abandoned.

Within the Russian Arctic there are four military airfields on the Arctic islands and a few more on the mainland; until autumn 2018 there was no permanent air unit at any of them. The airfields on the islands (all under Northern Fleet jurisdiction) comprise Rogachevo on Novaya Zemlya (New Land) Island, Nagurskoye in the Franz Josef Land archipelago, Sredniy in the Severnaya Zemlya (Northern Land) archipelago and Temp on Kotelny Island in the

Seen after undergoing overhaul, Tu-142MK '95 Black' *Cherepovets* belongs to the the 5th Independent ASW Aviation Squadron at Kipelovo. (Beriev)

New Siberian Islands. Apart from Rogachevo, where a fighter regiment is to be deployed after lengthening of the runway to 3,000m (9,843ft), the remaining airfields on the Arctic islands receive only An-26 and An-72 light transport aircraft and helicopters.

Airfields on the Russian mainland are far more well established; usually these are the airports of neighbouring towns. On the mainland within the Arctic region, Russian military aviation uses airfields at Vorkuta (Northern Fleet), Naryan-Mar (Northern Fleet), Tiksi (Northern Fleet), Alykel (Central MD) and Anadyr (Eastern MD).

The deployment of combat air units to the Arctic was announced as early as 2014. The then commander-in-chief of the VVS Viktor Bondaryev said that tactical combat aircraft and MiG-31 interceptors would be based at Tiksi; he added: 'MiG-31s will also be based at Anadyr airfield'. Bondaryev gave a deadline of 2017 but this has not been met. Other sources have revealed plans for deploying a fighter regiment to Rogachevo airfield. At a meeting of a defence ministry board on August 31, 2018, Sergey Shoygu said that 'until the end of the year, the Northern Fleet will receive [...] 15 aircraft'. A MiG-31 was shown in the accompanying picture. As of December 2018 there was no information as to where these aircraft were deployed.

The airfields in the Arctic are also used by Russian Long-range Aviation as so-called forward airfields (see Long-Range Aviation on page 52).

MA VMF direct reporting units

Formation	Unit	HQ/Location	Inventory/Notes
859 TsBP PLS MA		Yeysk	
	190 USAP	Yeysk	Various naval aircraft
	Unknown AEPSO	Ostafyevo (Shcherbinka)	An-12, An-26, An-72, An-140

MA VMF aviation units assigned to the Northern Fleet/45th Air Force and Air Defence Army

Formation	Unit	HQ/Location	Inventory
Unknown KIAD		Severomorsk (?)	
	100 KIAP	Severomorsk-3	MiG-29KR/KUBR (2 sqn)
	279 KIAP	Severomorsk-3	Su-25UTG/Su-30SM (1 sqn), Su-33 (2 sqn)
98 OSAP		Monchegorsk	MiG-31BM (1 sqn), Su-24M (1 sqn), Su-24MR (1 sqn)
7050 AvB		Severomorsk-1	Il-38/Il-38N (1 sqn), Ka-27/Ka-27M (1 sqn), Mi-8/Ka-27PS/Ka-29 (1 sqn), transports (1 sqn)
	5 OPLAE	Kipelovo (Fedotovo)	Tu-142MK/Tu-142MR (1 sqn)
216th (?) OP BLA		Severomorsk-1	Forpost UAV

Northern Fleet HQ

I Severomorsk

MA VMF Bases

1 Yeysk
2 Ostafyevo (Shcherbinka)
3 Kipelovo
4 Monchegorsk
5 Severomorsk-3
6 Naryan-Mar
7 Rogachevo
8 Vorkuta
9 Nagurskoye
10 Alykel
11 Sredniy
12 Tiksi
13 Temp
14 Anadyr

Key

Naval Aviation HQ
MA VMF Base

occupied territory

A map of MA VMF direct reporting units and the Northern Fleet. (Map by James Lawrence)

Naval Aviation of the Pacific Fleet

Morskaya aviatsiya Tikhookeanskogo flota (MA TOF)

HQ: Vladivostok
Chief of MA TOF: Colonel Dmitry Karpov

The Pacific Fleet is subordinate to the Joint Strategic Command of the Eastern Military District. The Pacific Fleet forces are divided between two main locations. Vilyuchinsk in Kamchatka is close to Petropavlovsk Kamchatsky, where a strategic nuclear-powered submarine base is located. Meanwhile, most surface ships and diesel-powered submarines are based in the Vladivostok area. Air unit deployment is connected with the locations of the naval forces' bases. The aviation regiment in Yelizovo protects Kamchatka, while the air base in Nikolayevka protects the Vladivostok area. The long-range Tu-142 ASW aircraft based at Mongokhto are 1,300km (808 miles) away from Petropavlovsk Kamchatsky and 900km (559 miles) from Vladivostok.

Planned creation of AF and AD Army

In early 2018 rumours began to circulate suggesting planned creation of a new Joint Strategic Command of the Pacific Fleet, and an air force and air defence army within the command, as was done with the Northern Fleet in 2015. The jurisdiction of the new army would encompass Kamchatka, Chukotka and the eastern part of the Russian Arctic. Later expansion to the west and south – the Sakhalin and Kuril Islands – is possible. The HQ would be located at Petropavlovsk Kamchatsky. The AF and AD army

One of Russia's very few land-based naval fighter units is the 317th Independent Composite Aviation Regiment at Yelizovo. While it has begun to receive MiG-31BMs, '26 Blue' has not been upgraded. (Russian MoD)

would consist of the current 53rd AD Division in Yelizovo (with one S-400 and Pantsir-S missile regiment and a radar regiment) and a new composite aviation division, which would be formed on the basis of the current 317th Composite Aviation Regiment, also based at Yelizovo. The 317 OSAP's squadrons would be expanded to regiment strength.

317th Independent Composite Aviation Regiment (317 OSAP)

HQ: Yelizovo (Petropavlovsk Kamchatsky)
Commanding officer: Colonel Gennady Mironenko

In 2009, all units based in Yelizovo, including the 317 SAP with Il-38s and Ka-27s, and the 865 IAP with MiG-31s were merged into the 7060th Aviation Base. In 2017 the base was transformed into a regiment, with the number 317. As of the end of 2018 the regiment had one squadron of ASW aircraft with around eight Il-38 aircraft (including two upgraded Il-38Ns) and a squadron of ASW helicopters with approximately 20 Ka-27 helicopters (including upgraded Ka-27Ms), a fighter squadron with around 10 MiG-31s (since 2018 replaced by upgraded MiG-31BMs; there are also around 20 non-airworthy fighters still present at the base) as well as a detachment of An-12 and An-26 transport aircraft and Mi-8 helicopters; in 2017 the regiment received its first Mi-8AMTSh-VA Arctic helicopter. Apart from these assets the regiment includes a UAV squadron with Forpost and Orlan-10 systems (the first UAV detachment was formed in 2014). Yelizovo air base has recently been reconstructed and has two parallel runways 3,550m (11,647ft) long and 60m (197ft) wide.

Il-38 RF-75332 is based at Nikolayevka, as part of the Pacific Fleet's 7062nd Aviation Base.
(Russian MoD)

7062nd Aviation Base (7062 AvB)

HQ: Nikolayevka
Commanding officer: Colonel Igor Kireyev

In 2009, units based at Nikolayevka were merged into the 7062nd Aviation Base, which currently has two squadrons – the first one with six or seven Il-38s (there are also around 10 non-airworthy Il-38s stored at the base) and the second with Ka-27, Ka-29 and Mi-8 helicopters. In November 2017 the base received six Ka-29 assault-transport helicopters overhauled by the Kumertau facility; previously the base had had no airworthy Ka-29 helicopters for many years. The runway at Nikolayevka is 2,800m (9,186ft) long and 55m (180ft) wide. Two independent squadrons stationed at other airfields are also assigned to the base: a transport squadron at Knevichi and an ASW squadron at Mongokhto. The base also maintains a duty post at Khorol airfield.

Unknown Independent Transport Aviation Squadron (OTAE)

Location: Knevichi (Artyom)

This is a squadron with around 10 An-12, An-26 and An-140-100 transport aircraft, serving the Pacific Fleet HQ. Knevichi is also the international airport for Vladivostok; it has two parallel runways 3,650m (11,975ft) long and 60m (197ft) wide.

Unknown Independent ASW Aviation Squadron (OPLAE)

Location: Kamennyi Ruchey (Mongokhto)
Commanding officer: Lieutenant Colonel Mikhail Yurov

Kamennyi Ruchey was once a major base for Soviet-era naval aviation, with several regiments stationed there. In April 2011, Tu-22M missile carriers were transferred to the air force's Belaya base. An independent squadron with around eight Tu-142MZ ASW aircraft and at least two Tu-142MR radio relay aircraft remained at Mongokhto. There are around eight non-airworthy Tu-142s parked at the base, some of them with-

An-26 '04 Red' is assigned to the 7062nd Aviation Base at Nikolayevka and operated by the subordinate Independent Transport Aviation Squadron at Knevichi.
(Russian MoD)

The 7062nd Aviation Base at Nikolayevka includes this Ka-27PS utility and search and rescue helicopter, RF-34145 '78 Red'. (Russian MoD)

out engines. The unit also has a detachment with two Ka-27PS rescue helicopters, an An-26 transport aircraft and a Mi-8 helicopter. Kamennyi Ruchey (stone creek) is the name of the airfield, after a nearby creek, while Mongokhto is the name of the nearest municipality; Mongokhto means 'the dead forest' in Orochs, the local indigenous language. The base has a runway 3,400m (11,155ft) long and 60m (197ft) wide.

This Tu-142MZ-2 is on strength with the Independent ASW Aviation Squadron at Mongokhto, which also answers to the 7062nd Aviation Base. (Russian MoD)

Naval Aviation of the Pacific Fleet

Formation	Unit	HQ/Location	Inventory
317 OSAP		Yelizovo (Petropavlovsk Kamchatsky)	Il-38 (1 sqn), Ka-27 (1 sqn), MiG-31 (1 sqn), Forpost UAV (1 sqn), transports (1 det)
7062 AvB		Nikolayevka	Il-38 (1 sqn), Ka-27/Ka-29/Mi-8 (1 sqn)
	Unknown OTAE	Knevichi (Artyom)	An-12/An-26/An-140-100 (1 sqn)
	Unknown OPLAE	Kamennyi Ruchey (Mongokhto)	Tu-142MZ/Tu-142MR (1 sqn), transports (1 det)

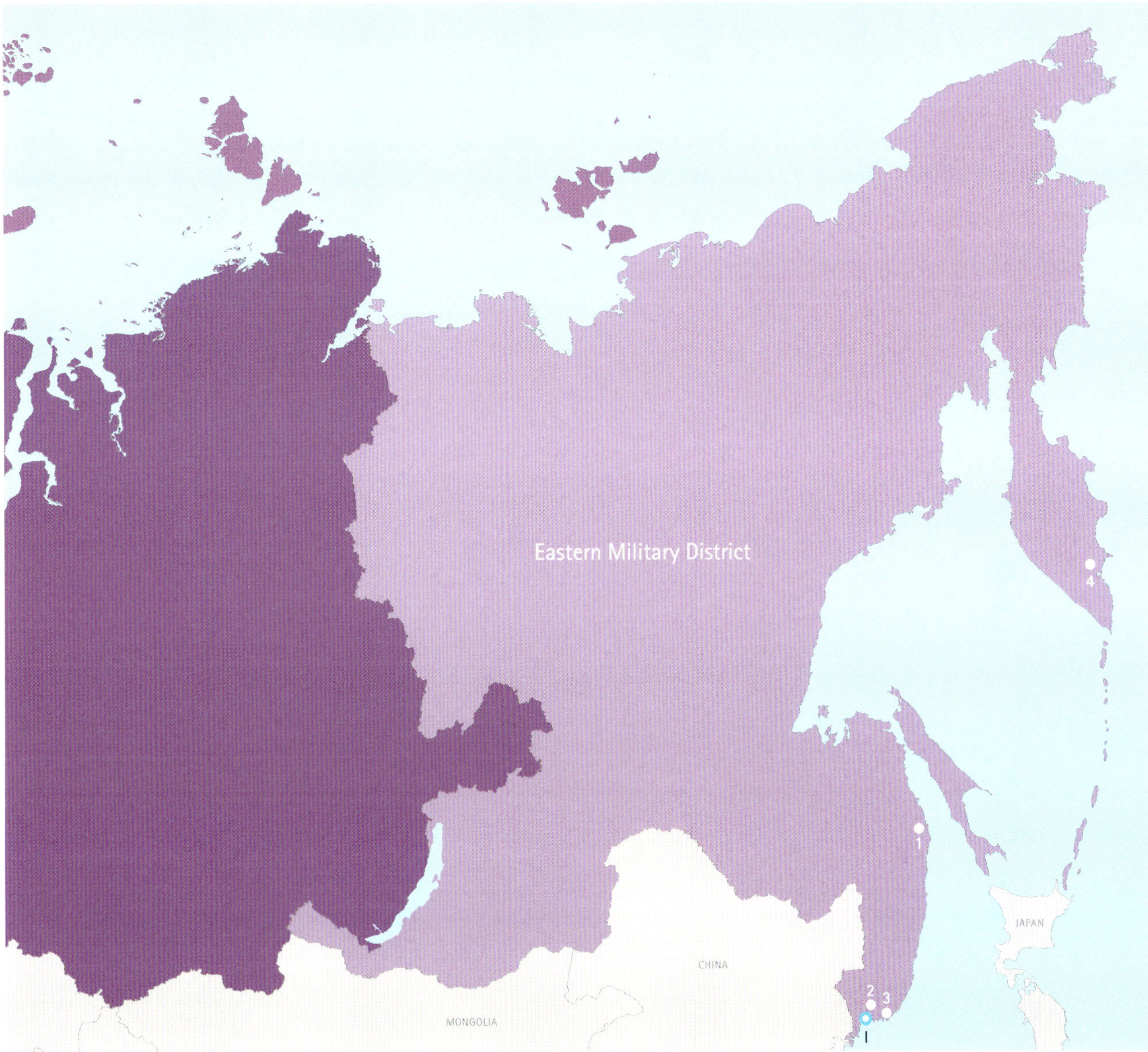

Pacific Fleet HQ

I Vladivostok

MA VMF Bases

1 Kamennyi Ruchey (Mongokhto)
2 Knevichi (Artyom)
3 Nikolayevka
4 Yelizovo (Petropavlovsk Kamchatsky)

Key

Naval Aviation HQ
MA VMF Base

A map of the Naval Aviation of the Pacific Fleet. (Map by James Lawrence)

Naval Aviation of the Baltic Fleet

Morskaya aviatsiya Baltiyskogo flota (MA BF)

HQ: Kaliningrad
Chief of MA BF: Colonel Andrey Kosterin

The Baltic Fleet is subordinate to the Joint Strategic Command of the Western Military District. All naval aviation assets of the Baltic Fleet are based in the Kaliningrad District.

72nd Aviation Base (72 AvB)

HQ: Chkalovsk
Commanding officer: Colonel Sergey Saushkin

In October 2010 all aviation assets of the Baltic Fleet were merged into the 7054th Aviation Base with its HQ in Chkalovsk. In June 2011, in the next wave of reorganisation, only a Ka-27 helicopter squadron and transport aircraft were left with naval aviation and were grouped into the 72nd Aviation Base. The Su-24 and Su-27 combat aircraft, as well as Mi-8 and Mi-24 helicopters, were subordinated to the Russian Air Force and incorporated as aviation groups within the 7000 AvB. This lasted for two years; in December 2013 they returned to the naval aviation control and were incorporated into the 72 AvB as attack, fighter and helicopter squadrons, respectively.

The detachment of transport aircraft at Chkalovsk, which serves the Baltic Fleet's command, includes several An-26 and Tu-134 aircraft; new An-140 and An-148 staff transport aircraft are expected.

A Forpost UAV in use with the Baltic Fleet in March 2018. (Russian MoD)

Modernisation of the Baltic Fleet's aviation component is being spearheaded by the multirole Su-30SM, including RF-34011 '73 Blue'. (Piotr Butowski)

Since the end of 2016 the Baltic Fleet has received new aircraft, leading to further organisational changes; the attack squadron had been expanded into the 4 MShAP regiment, while the fighter squadron has become the 689 IAP regiment. Numerous traditions of the 72 AvB, the Guard and Novogrod-Klaipeda titles, Air Marshal Ivan Borzov name and Red Banner order, were taken from the 4 OMShAP during reorganisations.

4th Naval Attack Aviation Regiment (4 MShAP)
Location: Chkalovsk

This regiment was formed on 17 April 1938. After World War II it remained in Eastern Prussia: from 1945 until 2018 it was continuously stationed at Chernyakhovsk. As a result of transformations during 2009–17, the regiment was downsized to a squadron; in 2017 it became the 4 MShAP regiment once again. In October 2018 the regiment moved to Chkalovsk; Chernyakhovsk remained as a reserve airfield.

In 1974 the regiment became the first operational unit to receive new Su-24 tactical bombers. In 1998 it took over reconnaissance Su-24MRs from another disbanded regiment.

On 13 December 2016 the unit received its first Su-30SM fighters. Currently there are eight Su-30SMs and a dozen Su-24Ms within the regiment. Reconnaissance Su-24MRs were replaced in 2013 by a detachment of Forpost UAVs. On 10 October 2017 two pilots from the unit died in the crash of a Su-24M at Hmeimim air base in Syria.

689th Fighter Aviation Regiment (689 IAP)
Location: Chkalovsk

This regiment derives its traditions from one of the best known Soviet fighter units, the 16 IAP of Guards (the number was changed to 689 in 1949), with which the Soviet ace Alexander Pokryshkin fought during World War II. In 1989 the regiment received the name Pokryshkin. From 1952 the regiment was stationed in Nivenskoye and in 2002 moved to Chkalovsk on the outskirts of Kaliningrad; from 1992 the regiment has flown the Su-27. In 2010 the regiment was reduced to a squadron, and in 2019 became a regiment again, with the restoration of the traditional number 689. Since January 2019, additional Su-27 fighters have arrived in Chkalovsk from the 790 IAP in Khotilovo, where they are being replaced by Su-35s.

Between autumn 2012 and autumn 2018 Chkalovsk airfield was the subject of reconstruction; the Su-27 fighters were temporarily moved to Chernyakhovsk. After the completion of the next stages of reconstruction, including the extension of the runway from the current 3,000m (9,843ft) to 3,500m (11,483ft) (these works began in summer 2018), and the addition of further aircraft parking stands and buildings, Chkalovsk airfield will be able to accommodate up to 100 aircraft.

Unknown Independent Shipborne ASW Helicopter Squadron (OKPLVE)
Location: Donskoye
Commanding officer: Lieutenant Colonel Aleksey Komarov

This squadron was established in 1955 near Baltiysk with Mi-4 helicopters; in 1958 it was moved to Donskoye. In 1961 the unit was subordinated to the navy as the 745th ASW Helicopter Regiment with Ka-15 helicopters; since 1988 the unit has operated Ka-27 and Ka-29 helicopters. In 1994 the regiment was reduced to a squadron, the 396 OKPLVE; it is possible is still bears this number. In November 2017 four Ka-29s, returned to service after many years of inactivity, arrived in Donskoye (one crashed in April 2018).

In January 2018 the first upgraded Ka-27M ASW helicopter arrived; to date, seven have been delivered.

Unknown Independent Helicopter Squadron (OVE)
Location: Donskoye

This unit was formed on 20 December 1976 as the 288 OVP, a regiment with Mi-8 and Mi-24 helicopters; from 1978 it was stationed in Nivenskoye near Kaliningrad. In 2002 the 288 OVP was reduced to a squadron, the 125 OVE, and redeployed first to Chkalovsk and then, in 2012, to Donskoye. In 2010 the squadron was assigned to the 7054th and subsequently the 72nd Aviation Base; it is possible is still bears the number 125. The squadron has around 10 Mi-24VP and Mi-8T helicopters.

MA VMF aviation units assigned to the Baltic Fleet

Formation	Unit	HQ/Location	Inventory
72 AvB		Chkalovsk	
	4 MShAP	Chkalovsk	Su-24M (1sqn), Su-30SM (1 sqn), Forpost UAV (1 det)
	689 IAP	Chkalovsk	Su-27 (2 sqn)
	OKPLVE	Donskoye	Ka-27/Ka-27M, Ka-29
	OVE	Donskoye	Mi-8, Mi-24

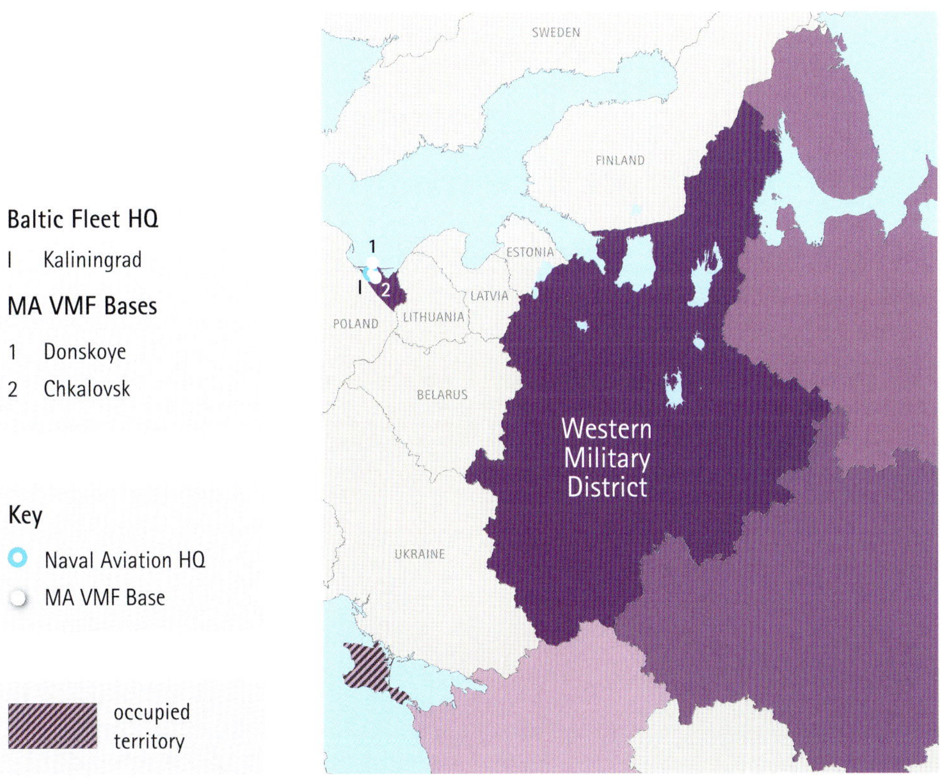

A map of the Naval Aviation of the Baltic Fleet.
(Map by James Lawrence)

Naval Aviation of the Black Sea Fleet

Morskaya aviatsiya Chernomorskogo flota (MA ChF)

HQ: Sevastopol (Crimea, Ukraine)
Chief of MA ChF: Colonel Sergey Bondaruk

After the breakup of the USSR, Russia and Ukraine divided the Black Sea Fleet between themselves; Ukraine agreed to the temporary stationing of the Russian Black Sea fleet in the territory of Crimea. Before 2014 all aviation assets of the fleet were based in Crimea and grouped into the 7057th Aviation Base at two locations: the Su-24 attack aircraft and Su-24MR reconnaissance aircraft were based at Gvardeyskoye, while Ka-27 ASW helicopters, a handful of Be-12 amphibians, and transport aircraft were based at Kacha.

After the seizure of Crimea in 2014, Russia has formed various new military units here, including a composite air force division. The navy has received new submarines and surface combatants. In naval aviation, the same two units have remained, but the combat aircraft have been transferred from Gvardeyskoye to Saki. The Black Sea Fleet is subordinate to the Joint Strategic Command of the Southern Military District. The Caspian Sea Flotilla, subordinated to the same Southern MD, is presented on page 116.

43rd Independent Naval Attack Aviation Regiment (43 OMShAP)

Location: Saki
Commanding officer: Colonel Andrey Kiselyov

After the breakup of the USSR, the 43 OMShAP with its 22 Su-17M3 (replaced in 2000 by Su-24) aircraft based at Gvardeyskoye was assigned to Russia and the base was leased from Ukraine. In 2011 the unit became an attack squadron within the 7057 AvB.

A pair of Su-30SMs – '43 Blue' and '45 Blue' – from the Saki-based 43rd Independent Naval Attack Aviation Regiment. (Piotr Butowski)

Su-24MR '16 White' is flown by the 43rd Independent Naval Attack Aviation Regiment, which moved to Saki in Crimea from Gvardeyskoye. (Piotr Butowski)

In 2014 the squadron was transformed back into the 43 OMShAP and moved to Saki. During 2015–16 the regiment received 12 Su-30SM fighters; the regiment's other squadron has six Su-24M and six Su-24MR aircraft. The runway at Saki air base is 3,200m (10,499ft) long.

318th Independent Composite Aviation Regiment (318 OSAP)

Location: Kacha (Sevastopol)
Commanding officer: Colonel Anatoly Stepanov

In 2009 the transport aircraft, Be-12 amphibians and Ka-27 helicopters based at Kacha were grouped into the 7057 AvB, renamed the 318 OSAP in July 2014. The regiment has one ASW helicopter squadron with Ka-27s, a transport and rescue squadron with An-26 aircraft and Ka-27PS and Mi-8 helicopters, as well as a handful of Ka-29 assault-transport helicopters and a few Be-12 amphibians. Kacha air base has a runway 2,000m (6,562ft) long and 40m (131ft) wide. The regiment also has a Forpost UAV squadron, based at the neighbouring Khersones airfield. It is expected to be expanded to regiment strength in future.

Kacha is home to the Russian Navy's last Be-12 amphibians. Operator is the 318th Independent Composite Aviation Regiment. (Russian MoD)

Caspian Sea Flotilla

Kaspiyskaya Flotilla

HQ: Astrakhan

This is the dominant naval force on the Caspian Sea, operating around 30 small warships and approximately 50 auxiliary vessels. The main strike force consists of a handful of ships armed with Kalibr cruise missiles with a range of 1,500km (932 miles), capable of engaging targets in Central Asia and the Middle East, as demonstrated by the attacks on Syria.

The flotilla's only aviation assets are a detachment of two Mi-8 helicopters based at Kaspiysk airfield near Makhachkala.

MA VMF aviation units assigned to the Black Sea Fleet

Formation	Unit	HQ/Location	Inventory
43 OMShAP		Saki	Su-24M/Su-24MR (1 sqn), Su-30SM (1 sqn)
318 OSAP		Kacha (Sevastopol)	An-26/Mi-8 (1 sqn), Ka-27/Ka-29 (1 sqn), Be-12 (1 det)
	OE BLA	Khersones (Sevastopol)	Forpost UAV

MA VMF aviation units assigned to the Caspian Sea Flotilla

Formation	Unit	HQ/Location	Inventory
		Kaspiysk	Mi-8 (det)

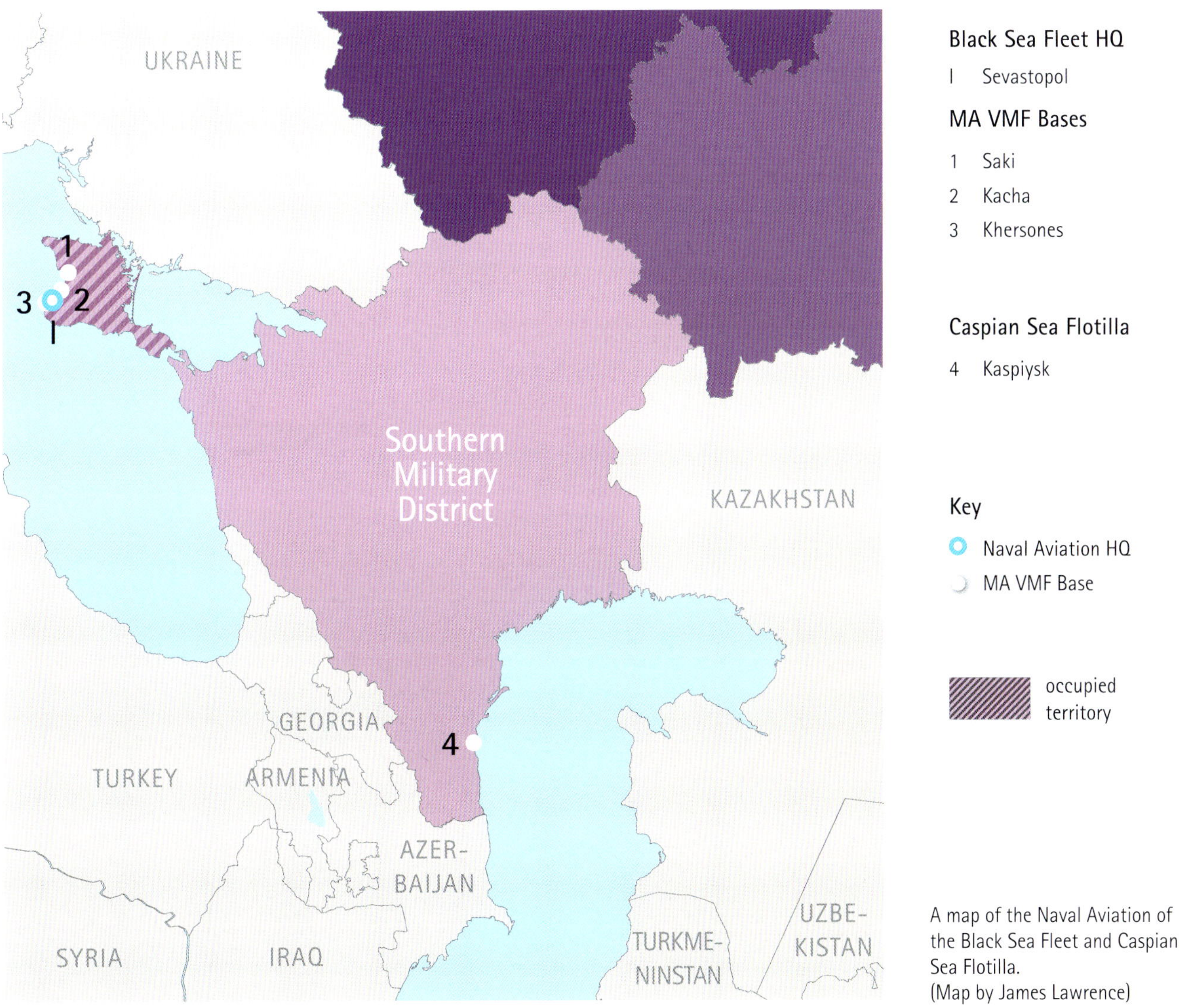

A map of the Naval Aviation of the Black Sea Fleet and Caspian Sea Flotilla. (Map by James Lawrence)

Aviation assets of the Federal National Guard Service

The **Federal National Guard Service** (Federalnaya sluzhba Voysk Natsionalnoy gvardii Rossiyskoy Federatsii, or Rosgvardia) was created by a presidential decree of 5 April 2016 from the former Interior Troops of the Ministry of Internal Affairs, and incorporating various law-enforcement agencies. A total of 340,000 military and civilian personnel serve in Rosgvardia. It is headed by Vladimir Putin's former chief bodyguard, Viktor Zolotov. Rosgvardia's aviation department is headed by Lieutenant General Alexander Afinogentov (since 2012). Rosgvardia'a aviation day is 3 March; on that day in 1978 the first unit, the 1 OAE of the Ministry of Internal Affairs, was formed in Khabarovsk.

Territorially, the Federal National Guard Service is divided into seven districts, in which aviation regiments and squadrons are based. An aviation squadron of Rosgvardia typically has six Mi-8 helicopters (mainly the Mi-8MTV-2 version) and sometimes also one to three heavy Mi-26 helicopters. The composite squadron based at Khabarovsk has an additional pair of An-26 aircraft, while the composite squadron based at Chkalovsky, which serves Rosgvardia's HQ, also has a few An-72, Tu-134, Tu-154 and Yak-42 passenger aircraft. Two regiments also operate Il-76 heavy transport aircraft. Rosgvardia is the main structure responsible for counter-insurgency operations in the North-

Operating from Voronezh, this is Mi-8MTV-2 RF-34280 '120 Yellow' from Rosgvardia's 11th Independent Aviation Squadron. (Rosgvardia)

Rosgvardia's most capable transport asset is the Il-76MD This is RF-76828 from the 675 Independent Composite Aviation Regiment at Nizhny Novgorod. (Piotr Butowski)

ern Causasus; two regiments operating in that region (Rostov-on-Don and Mozdok) are equipped with Mi-24 attack helicopters.

Additionally, within Rosgvardia's regional departments (one level lower than a district) are the **Aviation Detachments of Special Purpose** (Aviatsionnyi Otryad Spetsialnogo Naznacheniya, AOSN); there are more than 40 such detachments scattered

Mi-8AMT RF-28984 takes part in anti-terror excercises with the *Sovetsky Soyuz* icebreaker in April 2018. (Rosgvardia)

Anonymous-looking Sukhoi Superjet RF-89151 is part of the Rosgvardia fleet and is used for the rapid deployment of counter-terror teams. (Piotr Butowski)

throughout the entire territory of Russia. The primary equipment of the AOSNs are UAVs; some also have an Ansat, Ka-226 or Mi-8 helicopter.

The exception is AOSN Yastreb (hawk), subordinated to the **Special Purpose Centre of Rapid Response Forces and Aviation of Rosgvardia** in Chkalovsky (Shcholkovo), which operates a Sukhoi Superjet passenger aircraft (used for transport of Rosgvardia's rapid response combat team, not executives), a Mi-8 helicopter, two AS355N Ecureuil helicopters and UAVs.

The primary aviation equipment of Rosgvardia are Mi-8 medium helicopters (more than 100), Mi-26 heavy helicopters (around 10), light Ansat and Ka-226 helicopters (around a dozen) and Mi-24 combat helicopters (approximately eight).

Rosgvardia's helicopters are marked with a white stripe around the tail boom. Fixed-wing aircraft comprise around ten Il-76 heavy transport aircraft and 10 light An-26 transport aircraft as well as single aircraft of other types. Rosgvardia operates three types of lightweight (up to 10kg; 22lb) UAVs made by the Russian ZALA company (models 421-08, 421-16E and 421-21), as well Oko (eye) aerostats for fixed observation posts.

In June 2017 General Afinogentov presented plans for the renewal of Rosgvardia's air fleet to 'increase the portion of modern aircraft to 70 per cent by 2025'. Rosgvardia is due to receive new versions of the Mi-8AMT and AMTSh transport helicopters, Mi-26T2 heavy helicopters and Mi-35M attack helicopters. The replacement of the An-26 light transport by new Il-112, and the heavy Il-76 transport by new Il-76MD-90A is planned, as is the purchase of An-148 and Tu-204 passenger aircraft.

In November 2017 Rosgvardia received its first new aviation equipment for many years: three Mi-8AMTSh helicopters were delivered to the regiment in Mozdok; the next helicopters of this version were delivered to Mozdok in 2018.

In July 2018 Rosgvardia received its first Ka-226T light helicopter; it was delivered to the Aviation Detachment of Special Purpose in Krasnoyarsk.

A detailed ORBAT table of all Federal National Guard Service units can be found on page 124.

Aviation assets of the Federal Security Service

The **Federal Security Service** (Federalnaya sluzhba bezopasnosti, FSB) is Russia'd principal security agency, responsible for internal and border security, counter-intelligence, counter-terrorism and investigating the most dangerous crimes. It is a successor to the USSR's Committee of State Security (KGB). Personnel strength of the FSB amounts to around 230,000, including 160,000 border guards.

The traditions of the FSB's aviation date back to 14 August 1923, when an order was issued to form the first five air squadrons of the Soviet secret police, the GPU; 14 August is marked as the holiday of FSB aviation. For many years, the present-day FSB aviation served the border guard, first within the KGB, then during 1993–2003 as the independent Federal Border Guard Service (Federalnaya pogranichnaya sluzhba, FPS), and since 2003 again within the FSB.

After 2003, FPS aviation was transformed into FSB aviation, used by all FSB structures, although most tasks are still related to border protection. Former regiments and squadrons from the border guard aviation were transformed into **Combined Aviation Detachments** (Obyedinyonnyi aviatsionnyi otryad, OAO FSB RF), based at several airfields, or **Independent Aviation Detachments** (Otdelnyi aviatsionnyi otryad, OAO FSB RF), each based at a single airfield; the Russian abbreviation OAO is the same in both cases.

In February 2000 an FSB aviation squadron was formed at Vnukovo airfield near Moscow with two Tu-134 and Tu-154 passenger aircraft and a handful of Mi-8 helicopters; the squadron's task was to rapidly deploy the FSB's special Alfa and Vympel groups. Now it is the Combined Aviation Detachment of Special Purpose of Aviation of FSB. The aviation of the FSB is managed by the **FSB Aviation Department** (Upravleniye aviatsii FSB) in Moscow.

A Mi-35M is inducted into service in the traditional manner with the FSB's Second Combined Aviation Detachment at Kochubeyevskoye in April 2018. (FSB)

Part of the FSB's Combined Aviation Detachment of Special Purpose at Moscow Sheremetyevo, An-72 RF-72010 was intercepted flying in Finnish airspace on 28 August 2014. (Finnish MoD)

The air fleet of the FSB consists of around 60 fixed-wing aircraft and some 130 helicopters. The fixed-wing aircraft are mainly An-26 (around 25) and An-72 (around 15, including some six An-72P) light transports, as well as a handful of An-148-100EA, heavy Il-76, Il-96-400VPU, Tu-134, Tu-214VPU passenger aircraft and Yak-18T trainers. The An-72P armed transport and patrol aircraft was developed specifically for the border guard. A few An-72Ps are assigned to the detachment in Yelizovo (Kamchatka); some are also at Yuzhno-Sakhalinsk and Danilovo.

In May 2016 the FSB placed an order for two Austrian-made Diamond Aircraft DA42M-NG aircraft fitted with reconnaissance equipment, to be delivered to Stavropolsky Krai by November 2017. There is no information as to whether they have been delivered.

The bulk of the helicopters operated by the FSB comprise around 80 Mi-8s; in addition, there are around 15 Ka-27PS helicopters (used on coastal sections of the border), fewer than 10 heavy Mi-26s, plus single Ansat and Ka-226 helicopters. The FSB also has five Mi-35M helicopters (delivered in April 2018 to the detachment at Stavropol) and similar number of older Mi-24s. The FSB also operates small UAVs and surveillance balloons.

The detailed ORBAT table of Federal Security Service can be found on page 124.

Vnukovo-based Mi-8MTV RF-23100, part of the FSB's Combined Aviation Detachment of Special Purpose, carries various additional antennas. (Piotr Butowski)

Aviation assets of the Federal Guard Service

The **Federal Guard Service** (Federalnaya sluzhba okhrany, FSO) is tasked with protection of high-ranking state officials including the president of Russia. It is a vast service with 40,000 to 50,000 personnel. The structure of the aviation assets operated by the FSO is unknown.

It is known that the service has three Mi-35MS helicopters and several special versions of Mi-8.

In November 2018 the FSO conducted a training exercise in the centre of Moscow with the participation of two Mi-8 helicopters; according to official information, 'anti-terrorist operations were practiced'.

Aviation regiments and squadrons of Rosgvardia

Subordination	Unit	Location	Approx. inventory
Main Staff of Rosgvardia	70 OSAP	Yermolino	An-12 (2), An-26 (5), Il-76 (4–5), Mi-8 (10), Mi-26 (1–2)
	3 OSAE	Chkalovsky (Shcholkovo)	An-72, Mi-8 (4), Tu-134 (2–3), Tu-154 (2–3), Yak-42
Central District	11 OAE	Voronezh	Mi-8 (6), Mi-26
North-Western District	7 OAE	Pushkin (St Petersburg)	Mi-8 (6)
Volga District	675 OSAP	Nizhny Novgorod	Il-76 (6), Mi-8 (6)
	8 OAE	Engels	Mi-8 (6)
North-Caucasus District	685 OSAP	Rostov-on-Don	An-26, Mi-8 (6), Mi-24 (4), Mi-26
	142 OSAP	Mozdok	Mi-8 (15, including AMTSh), Mi-24 (4), Mi-26
	6 OAE	Krasnodar	Mi-8 (6), some Ka-226
Ural District	9 OAE	Yekaterinburg	Mi-8 (6)
Siberian District	2 OAE	Irkutsk	Mi-8 (6)
	10 OAE	Novosibirsk	Mi-8 (10), Mi-26 (2–3)
Eastern District	1 OSAE	Khabarovsk	Mi-8 (6-8), An-26 (2)

Aviation units of the Federal Security Service

Unit	Location	Remarks
Aviation Base of FSB	Danilovo (Yoshkar-Ola)	
Combined Aviation Detachment of Special Purpose	Moscow Sheremetyevo	Aviation Groups at Vnukovo and Belgorod
Combined Arctic Aviation Detachment	Vorkuta	Aviation Groups at Tiksi, Murmansk, Khatanga and Chersky
First Independent Aviation Detachment	Besovets (Petrozavodsk)	
Second Combined Aviation Detachment	Mikhaylovsk (Stavropol)	Aviation Groups at Kochubeyevskoye and Khankala (Grozny)
Third Independent Aviation Detachment	Tolmachovo (Novosibirsk)	
Fourth Independent Aviation Detachment	Shagol (Chelyabinsk)	
Fifth Combined Aviation Detachment	Yelizovo (Petropavlovsk Kamchatsky)	Aviation Groups at Magadan and Bukhta Provideniya (Providence Bay)
Sixth Combined Aviation Detachment	Yuzhno-Sakhalinsk	Aviation Group at Mendeleyevo (Yuzhno-Kurilsk)
Seventh Independent Aviation Detachment	Vladivostok Knevichi	
Eighth Independent Aviation Detachment	Khabarovsk Tsentralnyi	
Ninth Independent Aviation Detachment	Chita Cheryomushki	
Tenth Independent Aviation Detachment	Makhachkala Uytash	
Eleventh Independent Aviation Detachment	Adler (Sochi)	

Note: Numbers in unit names are written in words.

Rosgvardia Bases

1 Krasnodar
2 Rostov-on-Don
3 Mozdok
4 Voronezh
5 Yermolino
6 Chkalovsky
7 Pushkin
8 Nizhny Novgorod
9 Engels
10 Yekaterinburg
11 Novosibirsk
12 Irkutsk
13 Khabarovsk

FSB Bases

1 Adler (Sochi)
2 Mikhaylovsk (Stavropol)
3 Makhachkala
4 Besovets
5 Danilovo
6 Shagol (Chelyabinsk)
7 Tolmachovo (Novosibirsk)
8 Chita Cheryomushki
9 Khabarovsk Tsentralnyi
10 Vladivostok Knevichi
11 Yuzhno-Sakhalinsk
12 Yelizovo (Petropavlovsk Kamchatsky)
13 Moscow-Sheremetyevo
14 Vorkuta

Key

● Rosgvardia Base
● FSB Base
occupied territory

A map showing the aviation units of Rosguvardia and the Federal Security Service. (Map by James Lawrence)

MILITARY AIRCRAFT ACQUISITION POLICY

The turn of this century was the toughest period for modern Russian aviation. Russia faced economic turbulence and made drastic cuts to military spending. The air force lacked money for fuel or aircraft overhauls. The deputy commander-in-chief of VVS for procurement, Major General Dmitry Morozov complained in August 2003 that the aircraft airworthiness rate in the air force was at 50 per cent. Deliveries of new aircraft had eventually come to a halt nearly 10 years earlier.

The rebound began around 2000, when Russia recovered from the financial collapse of August 1998. At that time a sustained increase in oil prices – the main driver of the Russian economy – began on the world markets; starting with USD20 per barrel, in February 2008 the oil price exceeded USD100 per barrel for the first time in history. After a decade-long recess, Russia began to refresh its air force inventory. This began with modest upgrades for combat aircraft, and in 2005 the defence ministry placed its first orders for new aircraft (18 Su-34s and 12 Yak-130s) and helicopters (67 Mi-28Ns). A flurry of orders fllowed in the years to come.

The Su-34 production line in Novosibirsk.
(UAC)

Flight hours

At the beginning of the new millennium, levels of pilot training became critically low. For instance, in 2001 a fighter pilot logged 14 flight hours, the pilot of a Su-25 attack aircraft 20 hours, the pilot of a Su-24 tactical bomber 13 hours, the pilot of a strategic bomber 20 hours; transport pilots improved the average with their flight time of 50 hours. The level of pilot training and rate of aircraft airworthiness were not evenly distributed: in selected permanent alert units the flight time was several times higher than the average and almost satisfied the minimum requirements for sustaining combat readiness. In the remaining regiments only some pilots (the first squadron) were flying. In naval aviation as many as 43 per cent of pilots logged only two to three flight hours a year; 27 per cent logged 10 to 20 hours, and 30 per cent recorded around 50 hours.

In 2002 an improvement in pilot training began, slow at first (for instance, 39 flight hours in 2006), and then faster (90 hours in 2011).

Currently the average Russian pilot logs around 100 flight hours per year; less in tactical aviation, but more in long-range and transport aviation (120 flight hours).

What is the State Armament Programme?

The State Armament Programme (Gosudarstvennaya programma vooruzheniya, GPV) is a document setting out plans for purchase, repairs and upgrades, as well as research and development of weapons and other military equipment. The GPV is adopted for 10 years, of which the first five years are detailed, and the second more general. The next programme is adopted after five years, resulting in five years 'overlap'.

Coordination of activities for the formation and substantiation of the GPV is assigned to the defence ministry. The actual drafting of the GPV programme is the responsibility of the **46th Central Research Institute of the Ministry of Defence** (TsNII MO RF) in Moscow, headed by Colonel (ret.) Sergei Bokov. The TsNII VVS MO RF in Shcholkovo takes part in the creation of the aviation elements of the programme. The GPV is a multi-volume document concerned with armaments and other military equipment, accompanied by background technical and financial documentation. The GPV is complementary to other state programmes including the State Programme for the Development of the Defence Industrial Complex, which sets out tasks for the development of arms production facilities and their tooling.

What is the State Defence Order?

The GPV does not have the force of law and does not result directly in orders for the arms industry. It can also be subject to frequent amendment in the course of its implementation. The GPV is implemented through the State Defence Order (Gosudarstvennyi oboronnyi zakaz, GOZ) and only the GOZ is a firm order.

The permanently functioning body formulating the GOZ and controlling its implementation is the Military-Industrial Commission (Voyenno-promyshlennaya komissiya, VPK). President of Russia Vladimir Putin is the head of the VPK; his deputy is Yuri Borisov, the deputy prime minister of the Russian government, responsible for the arms industry.

Previously GOZ contracts were signed for one year, but they have been extended to three or four years, which allows the industry to work more stably. On signing a contract, the defence ministry makes a pre-payment of 50 to 80 per cent of the value of the contracts, which also stabilises the industry. On the other hand, the profitability of contracts for the Russian MoD is much lower than that of export contracts.

State Armament Programme for 2011–2020

On 31 December 2010 the State Armament Programme for 2011–2020 (GPV 2020) was adopted by the decree of the President of Russia Dmitri Medvedev. A total of 19.4 trillion roubles (equivalent to USD285 billion) was allotted for GPV 2020, including 24 per cent for the air force; the air force was to receive more than 600 new fixed-wing aircraft and more than 1,000 helicopters within 2011–20. The main quantitative criterion of the fulfilment of GPV 2020 is reaching a 70 per cent proportion of new equipment and weaponry in the armed forces by 2020; at the programme's start, this proportion amounted to 16 per cent. According to Sergey Shoygu's report, 61 per cent had been reached by the end of 2018 across the entire armed forces, including 64 per cent for the VVS and 74 per cent for the VKS (the average in the VKS is increased by the Space Troops).

The programme was implemented without delays until 2015. Fixed-wing aircraft deliveries for the Russian MoD increased quickly from 19 aircraft in 2011, to 35 in 2012, 54 in 2013, 103 in 2014, and 93 in 2015. Helicopter deliveries were at a level of 100 to 120 per year. After 2014 a slump was caused by a drop in oil prices and Western sanctions after the invasion of Ukraine. Yuri Borisov said in December 2018 that at that time the MoD was receiving 50 to 60 fixed-wing aircraft and 30 to 40 helicopters per year; Russia had stopped disclosing the exact numbers. The official explanation given by Borisov was that purchases were reduced because 'saturation had occurred' and there was no need for more, but the facts are different. The production plans announced earlier by UAC and Russian Helicopters provided for deliveries of 100 to 105 fixed-wing aircraft and 150 to 160 helicopters per year to the Russian MoD during the final years of implementation of the GPV 2020. A particularly severe collapse occurred in the production of helicopters, and particularly the Mi-8. Here the lack of money overlapped with engine shortages; the TV3-117 engines are manufactured in Ukraine and Russian production of VK-2500 is still insufficient.

Su-25SM3 '05 Red' on the repair and modernisation line at the ARZ 121 in Kubinka in 2018. (Piotr Butowski)

Preparing for new production, the factory in Kazan completed one of two Tu-160 airframes which remained there from the Soviet period. The new Tu-160 named *Pyotr Deynekin* is the 35th of this type in total; it was first flown in December 2017. (UAC)

In the mid-2000s Russia launched mid-life upgrade programmes for all combat aircraft types, but their fortunes varied. Mid-life upgrades for MiG-29 fighters ended at the test stage (MiG-29SMT fighters are in service, but these are new-production aircraft). Su-27SM upgrades ended after 48 aircraft had been upgraded (plus a few Su-27SM3 versions). Both the MiG-29 and Su-27 are simply being replaced by new fighters, the former by Su-30SMs and the latter by the Su-35S.

Much more successful was the outcome of the MiG-31BM interceptor and Su-25SM3 attack aircraft upgrades. In both cases not only are all examples of these types in service being modernised, but those preserved in storage are being brought back into service. The MiG-31 may be given new duties in the coming years; a squadron of MiG-31K aircraft with the Kizhal system is in the trials phase and a satellite interceptor version is being tested. The Su-24M SVP-24 upgrade is also highly praised. Upgrades of strategic bombers are being carried out; each year one or two Tu-160 and two to four Tu-95MS bombers are upgraded. Series upgrades of Tu-22M3Ms are to begin in 2021.

Rollout of the first modernised Tu-22M3M on 16 August 2018. The modernised bomber made its maiden flight at the Kazan Aviation Plant on 2 December the same year. (Tatarstan)

Aircraft delivered to the Russian MoD

Type	Number delivered	
	2001–10	2011–18
Combat aircraft and jet trainers		
MiG-29KR/KUBR	0	24
MiG-29SMT/UB	34	16
Su-27SM(3)	4	8
Su-30M2	2	18
Su-30SM	0	114
Su-34	7	112
Su-35S	0	78
Tu-160	1	0
Yak-130	9	100
Total	**57**	**469**
Transport and special duty		
An-140-100	0	9
An-148-100	0	15
DA42T	0	6
Il-76MD-90A	0	3
Il-96-400VVIP	0	1
L-410UVP-E20	0	approx. 20
Tu-214PU	0	2
Tu-214R/ON	0	4
Total	**0**	**approx. 60**
Helicopters		
Ansat-U	8	42
Ka-52	4	approx. 110
Ka-226V	0	42
Mi-8	approx. 30	approx. 300
Mi-35M	0	76
Mi-26	0	approx. 30
Mi-28N/UB	approx. 30	approx. 80
Total	**approx. 72**	**approx. 680**
Grand total	**approx. 129**	**approx. 1,209**

State Armament Programme for 2018–2027

Another GPV programme was to be formally adopted in 2015 to encompass the years 2016–25. However, the events of 2014 caused a radical change of Russia's economic parameters and the new GPV was adopted by President Vladimir Putin's decree as late as 14 December 2017; it encompasses the years 2018-27. Furthermore, the funds that Russia intended to allot for this programme were vanishing rapidly. First it was announced that the new GPV would cost 55 trillion roubles. In December 2014 Sergey Shoygu provided a new number – 30 trillion – and in the final approved version this is reduced to 19 trillion roubles. Formally, for the years 2018-27 the same money as in the previous decade was allotted. In fact, the Russian rouble lost half of its value relative to the US dollar during this period. The target of the GPV is to maintain 70 per cent of new equipment and armament in the Russian Armed Forces. According to Yuri Borisov, 70 per cent 'is a certain threshold at which it is considered that the armed forces are fully capable'.

Series production

The priority of the GPV 2027 are the strategic nuclear forces, a fact repeatedly declared by Russian officials, including Vladimir Putin. On the aviation side this is represented by the programme to resume Tu-160 series production in the 'deeply modernised' M2 version; it is the only programme that has been boosted after 2014. On 25 January 2018 the MoD placed an order for 10 new-production Tu-160M2 bombers. The first new production aircraft is due to fly in 2021.

On 22 August 2018 two other contracts were signed under the new GPV for the first, small batches of new fighters. The deputy defence minister for acquisitions Aleksey Krivoruchko and the UAC President Yuri Slyusar inked a contract for six MiG-35 and two Su-57 fighters. Orders for a total of 20 MiG-35s and 15 Su-57s within the next few years have been announced. When signing the contract, Aleksey Krivoruchko stated that the defence ministry expects the deliveries of 'second-stage' Su-57 fighters from 2023.

In the case of the Su-57, this is clearly a retrograde measure after earlier announcements of production of 60 fighters by 2020 and plans for a further 150–160 by 2025. The official position was explained in July 2018 by Russia's deputy prime minister

The improved Mi-28NM during tests. (Russian MoD)

Yuri Borisov who said in a TV interview that 'the Su-35 is considered one of the best aircraft in the world and therefore we have no reason today to force activities on mass production of the fifth-generation [Su-57] aircraft.' However, the true reasons for the reduction of the expected Su-57 purchases can be traced back to shortcomings in its current form and the much higher cost than current-production fighters.

From contracts signed in previous years by the Russian MoD, 20 Su-35S and 10 Su-34 aircraft are to be produced in 2019–20. After their delivery, older types remaining in the Russian Aerospace Forces inventory will comprise around 100 Su-24s (including approximately 40 Su-24MR reconnaissance versions), around 70 MiG-29s (half of which are MiG-29SMTs, not yet needing replacement) and some 80 Su-27s (60 of which are upgraded Su-27SM and SM3 aircraft). Naval Aviation will have some 30 Su-24M and 12 Su-27 aircraft to be replaced. Assuming renewal of the fleet on a 1:1 basis, the demand for tactical aircraft under GPV-2027 may be estimated at around 100 Su-34, 60 Su-30SM and 30 Su-35S aircraft; these numbers are much smaller than in the previous GPV. In the case of the Su-30SM and Su-34, orders will concern the upgraded versions of these aircraft.

In February 2019 Yuri Borisov announced at Arsenyev that the purchase of 114 upgraded Ka-52M helicopters was planned in the GPV 2027. A batch of upgraded Mi-28NM attack helicopters will be ordered from the Rostov-on-Don production facility. As early as December 2017, while visiting the UZGA plant in Yekaterinburg, Borisov announced the purchase of 35 Diamond DA42T aircraft assembled there, which will going be used as trainers; the first few aircraft were acquired in 2017–18. Alexey Krivoruchko said in August 2018 that the MoD would soon order the first batch of three Be-200 amphibians, with deliveries from 2019.

Transport aviation did not receive any new aircraft during the previous decade. The contract of 2012 for production of 39 Il-76MD-90A aircraft in Ulyanovsk failed, but the MoD has confirmed its intent to continue the project. Visiting Ulyanovsk in August 2018, Alexei Krivoruchko confirmed plans to order 14 new Il-78M90A aerial tankers (31 were mentioned a few years earlier). The gap in light transport aircraft is expected to be filled by 48 Il-112V aircraft; a maiden flight of the Il-112V was performed on 30 March 2019. A small batch of Beriev A-100 AEW&C aircraft will also be ordered. Series production of the first Russian medium-altitude, long-endurance UAV, the Orion (Inokhodets), will be launched.

The Il-78M-90A represents the first new aerial refuelling tanker for the Russian air arms for many years. (UAC)

Among air-launched weapons, strategic systems will again have priority. Production of the Kh-101 and Kh-102 missiles will be continued and a missile of even longer range, the Kh-BD Romans, will enter production. Production of the Kh-MTs (GZUR) hypersonic missile for heavy bombers will be launched.

Research and development work

Within the GPV 2027, priority will be given to those research and development projects that are at advanced stage. In tactical aviation, these comprise the 'second stage' Su-57 with new engines and the 20-tonne Sukhoi S-70 Okhotnik (hunter) unmanned combat air vehicle (UCAV); the S-70 demonstrator is expected to fly in 2019 at Akhtubinsk, where it was delivered in January from the factory in Novosibirsk. Totally new projects have been postponed to the end of decade or even beyond. In this group are the PAK DA Poslannik strategic bomber, PAK DP interceptor, STVST super-heavy-lift transport aircraft and new carrier-based PMKI fighter.

A significant slowdown of R&D work has occurred in Russia. The problems are much more serious than the simple lack of money after 2014. First of all, despite numerous attempts, the medium-level scientific and engineering cadre has not been restored after the previous collapse of the years 1990–2000. In a typical Russian R&D company (with few exceptions) there is a group of older employees at retirement age and younger employees who are still learning (and will probably not remain there long if there is no money and no interesting work).

Diversification means conversion

The Russian defence industry consists of 1,337 companies employing 2 million people (numbers given by Yuri Borisov in December 2018). Facing an unavoidable reduction of orders from the Russian MoD, many of these companies risk bankruptcy. Export might be the solution; around 21.4 per cent of the production output of the Russian arms industry, or USD14–15 billion per year, is exported. However, arms exports cannot be increased for several reasons. First, the Russian arms industry has increasingly less attractive offers; second, in August 2017 the United States passed the Countering America's Adversaries Through Sanctions Act (CAATSA), which discourages other nations from buying Russian hardware.

The Sukhoi S-70 Okhotnik UCAV began taxi trials in winter 2018-19.

Increasing civilian production in Russian arms production facilities will be one solution (in 2017 its proportion was 17.2 per cent). In January 2018 Vladimir Putin assinged the task of increasing the proportion of civilian production to 30 per cent by 2025 and 50 per cent by 2030. He ordered a detailed plan of who will produce what and deliver it to whom; state-owned enterprises will be forced to buy these products. Like every attempt to manage the economy by administrative means, such a move cannot succeed in the longer term. In Russia this programme is officially called 'diversification', to avoid associations with a similar programme of 'conversion' of the defence industry in early 1990s – one that ended in total failure.

APPENDIX 1: STRUCTURE BASICS

The primary tactical element in Russian military aviation is the **pair** (para) of aircraft, which is by definition inseparable and conducts combat tasks jointly. One of the aircraft is the leader (vedushchiy), who assesses the situation, assigns targets and leads the attack; the other is the wingman (vedomyi), tasked with escorting the leader or conducting the attack along with them. Two pairs form a **flight** (zveno). In long-range bomber aviation and transport aviation there is no division into pairs, and the equivalent of the flight is the **detachment** (otryad), consisting of three aircraft.

Three flights/detachments form an **aviation squadron** (aviatsionnaya eskadrilya). Additionally, within the squadron there is also the squadron commander's aircraft (in heavy aviation) or a pair of two-seat combat trainer aircraft (in tactical aviation). Typically, a bomber or transport squadron has 10 aircraft (three three-aircraft detachments and the commander's aircraft), or 12 in fighter aviation (three four-aircraft flights) and sometimes two additional combat trainers. In squadrons of two-seat combat aircraft, such as the MiG-31 or Su-34, there are no additional trainer aircraft.

Aviation regiment

The **Aviation regiment** (aviatsionnyi polk) is the basic independent organisational unit in the structure of Russian military aviation. The regiment is permanently based at one airfield and usually is its only user. A combat regiment usually has a reserve airfield near the permanent base, where a small duty post is maintained, plus a training area.

The **regiment commander** (komandir polka) is a senior officer, usually with the rank of colonel, and less often lieutenant colonel. The regiment commander commands the combat sub-units (aviation squadrons), having his deputies, regiment staff and chiefs of services. The deputy commanders manage flying training, aviation engineering service and doctrinal issues.

The **staff** (shtab) is a team of officers headed by the **chief of staff** (nachalnik shtaba), tasked with sustaining everyday combat capability of the regiment, combat mission planning, intelligence gathering, assessment of the enemy, etc. The chief of staff is also the regiment's commander first deputy. The intelligence, communications and radio support, electronic warfare, flight safety, navigational, search and rescue, parachute and meteorological services are subordinated to the chief of staff. The regiment commander, his deputies, sub-units' commanders, staff and chiefs of services are the **regiment management** (upravleniye polka).

Two pairs of aircraft form a flight (zveno). In this case, a flight of Su-24Ms. (Piotr Butowski)

The basic sub-units of an aviation regiment are the command post, flying operations management team and aircraft squadrons and flights. The **command post** (Komandnyi Punkt, KP) controls the actions of flight crews and sub-units and ensures contact with the higher commander and the interacting units. The **flying operations management team** (gruppa rukovodstva polyotami) controls the air traffic.

The aviation regiment has, in accordance with its complement, three aviation squadrons, i.e. 36 combat aircraft and up to six training aircraft within tactical aviation, and 30 aircraft in heavy bomber and transport aviation. The real strengths usually differ from the regular structures described above. Many regiments have only two squadrons. Especially in the case of older aircraft – overhauled, scrapped or transferred between units – squadrons may have fewer or more aircraft. Only in the case of new aircraft, delivered in batches direct from the production facility, does the strength comply with the regular structure.

Maintaining the aircraft and armament serviceability, diagnostics of the equipment's technical condition, aircraft cyclic maintenance and overhauls are the tasks of the **engineering aviation service** (Inzhenerno-aviatsionnaya sluzhba, IAS). This service is commanded by the deputy regiment commander for the IAS. They have at their disposal the IAS services of individual aviation squadrons, as well as facilities of the **technical operational unit** (Tekhniko-ekspluatatsionnaya chast', TECh), with specialists on individual systems.

The most numerous of the regiment's supporting sub-units are BATO, BS RTO and the sentry company. The **battalion of airfield and technical maintenance** (Batalyon Aerodromno-Tekhnicheskogo Obespecheniya, BATO) provides the maintenance of the airfield and its facilities, technical assistance to aircraft which have crashed, or emergency landed away from the airfield, etc. It supplies fuel, weapons, ammunition and other materiel to the aircraft. It also provides day-to-day deliveries of food and other kinds of support for the base personnel. The **battalion of communication**

In long-range bomber aviation the equivalent of a flight is the three-aircraft detachment (otryad) – represented here by Tu-22M3s.
(Piotr Butowski)

and radio support (Batalyon Svyazi i Radiotekhnicheskogo Obespecheniya; BS RTO) provides the aircraft with information necessary for take-off, navigation and landing approach by means of radio, lighting and communication systems. In the past, these used to be independent units (OBATO and OBS RTO respectively, where O stood for Odtelnyi, independent), stationed in the same garrison, but not subordinated to the aviation regiment commander. They lost independence in 2009, when the air bases were established, and have not regained it since, despite the transformation of the bases into regiments once again.

Parts of the regiment are also auxiliary services, such as medical service, radiation, chemical and biological protection service, automotive, weaponry, fuel and lubricant services, firefighting service, catering service, etc.

The personnel of an aviation regiment comprises around 900 to 1,200 servicemen (including 350 to 450 officers) and around 150 to 250 civilian employees. A large portion – around 400 servicemen – support sub-units, which until 2009 were not parts of the regiment. The aircrews – around 1.3 to 1.4 per aircraft – are exclusively career officers, graduates of military pilot or navigator schools.

Upper levels

Aviation regiments (usually three, but not necessarily), independent squadrons and auxiliary units are grouped into an **aviation division** (Aviatsionnaya Diviziya). The highest organisational level is the **air force and air defence army**, one per military district, comprising one to three aviation divisions, independent regiments and other units.

In Russian nomenclature the flight, detachment and squadron are **sub-units** (podrazdeleniye); the regiment is a **unit** (chast'); the division is a **tactical formation** (soyedineniye), and the army is a **strategic formation** (obyedineniye).

Army Aviation

The organisational scheme of army aviation (helicopter) units is similar to that of a fixed-wing aircraft regiment in respect of the command, staff and services. The complement of aviation squadrons is different. The basic unit of the army aviation is the **independent helicopter regiment** (Otdelnyi vertolotnyi polk, OVP) with three squadrons of 12 to 16 helicopters (three or four flights of four helicopters in each) and a handful of command or auxiliary helicopters. The regiment's lineup is mixed: two attack helicopter squadrons and one transport helicopter squadron or the opposite of this.

In 2013 the formation of **army aviation brigades** (Brigada Armeyskoy aviatsii, Br AA) began; the brigade is a tactical formation, i.e. equivalent to a division. The Br AA has two squadrons of attack helicopters (Ka-52, Mi-28N, Mi-35M) and two squadrons of combat-transport helicopters (Mi-8, Mi-26).

Additional terms

The term **independent** (Otdelnyi) denotes a unit situated one level higher in the command structure than its actual size. For instance, an independent squadron is equivalent to a regiment, although it may have only a couple or a dozen or so aircraft. Analogously, an independent regiment is placed in the command structure on a divisional level. 'Independents' are usually units performing specific tasks. For example, the aerial tanker regiment 203 OAP SZ based at Ryazan services all heavy bombers in Russia, therefore is subordinated directly to the Long-Range Aviation Command, not to one of the divisions. Independent formations are often reconnaissance or transport units, serving a high-level command.

The term **composite** (Smeshannyi) in a unit's name means the unit operates aircraft for various purposes. For instance, the 98th Composite Aviation Regiment in Monchegorsk operates a squadron of Su-24M bombers, a squadron of Su-24MR reconnaissance aircraft and a squadron of MiG-31BM interceptors.

The title **Guards** (Gvardeyskiy) was awarded to the most decorated units during World War II and still is the most prestigious title for Russian military units, scrupulously passed on along with other traditions during organisational changes (although sometimes also lost in the course of these changes). Along with the award of the Guard title, the unit number was changed; for instance, on 7 March 1942 the 6 IAP received the Guard title and a new number – 18 IAP of Guards (today it is the 18 ShAP Normandie-Niemen). In the past it sometimes occurred that two aviation regiments of the same number existed; one of Guards, the other not. For instance, the 22 IAP PVO (disbanded in 1992) was based in Bezrechnaya near Chita, and the 22 IAP of Guards (still extant) was in Tsentralnaya Uglovaya near Vladivostok.

APPENDIX 2: RUSSIA'S MILITARY AIRCRAFT INSIGNIA

National insignia used on Russia's military aircraft were approved by the government on 4 March 2010.

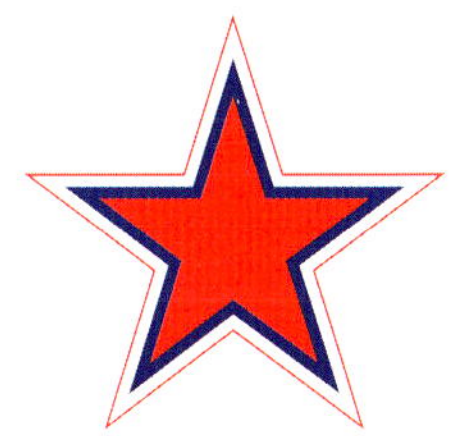

For aircraft and helicopters of the Russian Ministry of Defence and FSB the approved sign is the five-beam red star with an edging of blue and white, and the red line on a contour. The relation of the width of the blue and white bands to the diameter of the circle entered in a red field of the star is 1:10.

For aircraft of the Rosgvardia and FSO, the sign is a stylised image of the national flag of the Russian Federation, which represents a parallelogram consisting of three horizontal bands, white, blue and red. The relation of the length of the horizontal edge of a parallelogram to its height is 2:1. For contrast, a shading band of grey colour can be applied above and to right of the flag.

On the sides of naval aviation aircraft, the Russian Navy ensign known as the St Andrews's flag (adopted by a decree of the President of the Russian Federation on 21 July 1992) is applied. It has a white background with two blue diagonal bands, forming a saltire, known as the St Andrew's cross. The ratio of the flag's width to its length is 2:3, the width of the blue band is 1:10 the length of the flag.

In fact, markings do not always compliant to these rules. There are helicopters of Rosgvardia with markings in the form of a red star, probably not repainted after they were taken over from the Ministry of Internal Affairs. Meanwhile, on many military transport aircraft the marking is in the form of a flag, not a star.

Russian military aircraft wear two-digit (in training units sometimes three-digit) tactical numbers, usually red or blue with a thin white outline. Yellow or white numbers are rare. As a rule, aircraft of one unit wear numbers of the same colour; occasionally, when an aircraft is moved from one unit to another, for some time, it may keep the 'old' colours (for example, the 11 SAP in Marinovka has Su-24s with white and blue numbers). There are no strict rules to assigning these numbers. Usually, brand-new aircraft arrive from the production facility with successive numbers, but not necessarily. Known examples include one squadron with odd and the other with even numbers. One should not attach too much importance to these numbers since they may be changed. For instance, after their return from Syria the markings on many aircraft were revised.

The aircraft of the Ministry of Defence, Rosgvardia, FSB and FSO also have registrations consisting of the letters RF and five digits. Transport aircraft enrolled in the civil aviation register (for example the 223 or 224 LO) have the letters RA.

APPENDIX 3: NUMERICAL STRENGTH

Number of aircraft in Russian Aerospace Forces and Naval Aviation

Approximate numbers of fixed-wing aircraft and helicopters in active service as of the end of 2018 are listed below; aircraft in storage bases and derelict airframes were not counted.

A significant number of aircraft are in repair facilities and storage bases. Most will never be returned to service. However, in the case of some types, Russia may be interested in their overhaul combined with a thorough upgrade.

The MiG-31 has received a new lease of life; apart from the MiG-31BM upgraded interceptor version it has received new missions. Ten aircraft have been converted to the MiG-31K Kinzhal strike version as a carrier for the Iskander ballistic missile. A MiG-31 armed with a missile probably intended for destroying satellites is under test. Currently dozens MiG-31s are in storage and some may return to service in various applications.

The prototype of the upgraded Tu-22M3M bomber is undergoing flight evaluation since 28 December 2018. If Russia considers the upgraded aircraft has significant potential, some older aircraft may be overhauled and upgraded. Currently, several dozen non-airworthy Tu-22Ms are at storage bases and on various airfields (including around 25 at Olenyegorsk and about 20 at Belaya).

In 2016 Russia started to overhaul Ka-29 maritime assault helicopters, which had been in storage for over a decade. By the end of 2018 around 30 had been returned to service.

List of VKS aircraft in numbers

Aircraft role (total)	Type (quantity)
Heavy bombers (126)	Tu-22M (60), Tu-95MS (50), Tu-160 (16)
Tactical combat aircraft (795)	MiG-29 (70), MiG-31 (115, including 10 MiG-31K Kinzhal), Su-24M (70), Su-25 (140), Su-27 (100), Su-30M2 (20), Su-30SM (90), Su-34 (115), Su-35S (75)
AEW&C aircraft (10)	A-50/A-50U (10)
EW aircraft (46)	An-12PPS (3), Il-22PP (3), Mi-8 EW versions (40)

ISR aircraft (66)	An-30 (8), Il-20 (12), Su-24MR (40), Tu-22MR (2), Tu-214ON (2), Tu-214R (2)
C2 aircraft (21)	Il-22 (15), Il-80 (4), Il-82 (2)
Strategic transports and tankers (130)	An-22 (5), An-124 (10), Il-76 (100), Il-78 (15)
Theatre transports (212)	An-12 (65), An-26 (120), An-72 (25), Ka-27PS (2)
Passenger aircraft (97)	An-140 (5), An-148-100 (15), Il-62 (7), Il-96-400 (1), Tu-134 (50), Tu-154 (17), Tu-214 (3)
Trainers (518, these include fighter aircraft assigned to training bases)	An-2 (60), An-26 (10), Ansat (50), DA42T (6), Ka-226 (42), L-39C (120), L-410 (50), Mi-2 (30), MiG-29 (15), Su-25 (10), Su-27 (20), Tu-134 (10), Yak-130 (95)
Army helicopters (704)	Ka-52 (110), Mi-8 (300), Mi-24 (80), Mi-26 (40), Mi-28N (100), Mi-35M (74)

List of MA VMF aircraft in numbers

Aircraft role (total)	Type (quantity)
Fighters and attack aircraft (124)	MiG-29KR/KUBR (22), MiG-31 (24), Su-24M (30), Su-27 (12), Su-30SM (22), Su-33 (14)
ASW aircraft (42)	Be-12 (4), Il-38 (22), Tu-142MK/MZ (16)
AW&C/ISR/C2 aircraft and helicopters (20)	Ka-31R (2), Su-24MR (10), Tu-142MR (8)
Trainers (11)	L-39C (4), Su-25UTG (7)
Transport and passenger aircraft (61)	An-12 (5), An-26 (25), An-72 (10), An-140 (4), Il-18/Il-20/Il-22 (5), Tu-134 (10), Tu-154 (2)
Helicopters (131)	Ka-27 (70 ASW and 15 SAR versions), Ka-29 (30), Mi-8 (8), Mi-24 (8)